Your Memoirs

To Mae, without whom
my memoirs would not be much fun

Your Memoirs

*Collecting Them
for Fun and Posterity*

by
Seymour Rothman

McFarland & Company, Inc., Publishers
Jefferson, North Carolina, and London

Library of Congress Cataloguing-in-Publication Data

Rothman, Seymour, 1914–
  Your memoirs.

  Includes index.
  1. Autobiography. I. Title.
CT25.R68   1987   808'.06692   86-43086

ISBN 0-89950-267-9 (acid-free natural paper) ∞

Printed in the United States of America

McFarland   Box 611   Jefferson NC 28640

Table of Contents

Preface

The purpose of this book is to encourage you the reader to collect your memoirs, whether in bits and pieces or in a well-ordered manuscript, and preserve them for your children and grandchildren. They are your statement on what you were really like. Rest assured, they will become a family heirloom, and will be handed down from generation to generation.

Even though at the moment you haven't the slightest idea of what you would put in such collection, as you follow the suggestions in this book, memories will come pouring out. They're all in your head, and it's just a matter of unlocking them.

Memoirs are best told when they're told simply. You don't write them the way a professional would, you write them the way *you* would.

I. What Are Memoirs and Where Do They Come From?

An explanation of what you are getting into and what you will be getting out of writing your memoirs.

The question is, "What is a memoir?"

The answer is, "Virtually anything you care to put into writing for others to read."

The dictionary won't necessarily agree with this definition, but from the standpoint of putting together a set of memoirs (pronounced *mem-wahs* for reasons known only to the French) for posterity you can't beat it.

Memoirs are about you and life. Each has something to do with the life you've lived, the thoughts generated by it, or the lessons it taught you.

A memoir might come from a question. Someone asks what you think of suicide. Immediately you recall friends who might have considered that way out.

I once had a friend who was terminally ill, in pain when not drugged, and well aware of the futility of his life. I visited him frequently, and eventually we reached the point where we'd speak openly of his death. Frankly, it was the only subject that seemed to sustain his interest.

One day when we were being particularly frank, I said to

1

him, "I worry, Bob, that some day you will try to commit suicide."

"On, no," he replied. "I'll never do that. Living with death is a great adventure. I have to see how it comes out."

That is such a wonderful statement of the human spirit that it just has to be in someone's memoirs, even if they're only mine. At Bob's death I told the story to the minister, and he incorporated it in his eulogy. It brought a lot of comfort and understanding to all of us.

A memoir might be a statement of a home remedy for illness that you'd like to pass down through the ages.

Sore throat was a common illness when I was a little boy. Mom's cure was hot milk with sweet butter floating in it. I don't know why it worked, but it did. She'd bring the milk to my bedside, and when I finished she'd wrap a cold wet towel around my neck, and cover it with a dry towel to protect the bedclothing. I'd fall asleep, and when I'd awaken the sore throat would be gone.

I would have loved to try it later in life, but my inborn respect for the science of medicine prevented it. Instead I'd go through the expensive ritual of getting one shot and taking antibiotics for eight full days whether I needed them or not.

One of the memories that stayed with me through the years has to do with the first line of humor I ever wrote. It has significance for several reasons. For one, my newspaper career enjoyed the success that it did more because of my ability to write light features than to dig up heavy news. For another, it led to a lesson that could be very important to anyone dealing with youngsters.

The first line of humor I ever wrote was, "It is wiser to hit a small man on the head with a big hammer than to hit a big man on the head with a small hammer."

I believe I was in the third grade at the time, and the line was part of an assignment to demonstrate the division of paragraphs by writing three of them.

Humor magazines were very popular in those days, and the teacher decided that I had stolen the line from one of them. I don't know why this was important in an assignment like hers, but she asked me if I copied it from some magazine. I assured her I had not. I thought it up, and it struck me as being funny, I said.

Possibly it was the thought that I was lying to her that upset her. In any case she went into an angry lecture to the class about stealing someone else's work and misrepresenting.

I can't describe the shock of being so unjustly accused by such supreme authority, and having to sit by with no hope of combatting the disgrace and embarrassment being visited upon me.

My mother came to the school the next day to talk to the teacher, the first and only time she'd done that. I don't know what was said, but it made no difference to me. My frustration took the form of hatred for the teacher and the school, and it wasn't until the following year — when my writing efforts won some praise from the new teacher — that I once again could lose myself in the excitement of learning.

This turned out to be the first of many instances that convinced me that young people have a very strong sense of justice. Punish one for something he has done, and he accepts it and comes back ready and anxious to make peace. Punish him unjustly, however, and you have a sad and sullen youth, unforgiving, and difficult to deal with.

Here we have an example of a memory of an event that taught a lesson worth passing on, namely, children have a strong sense of justice and are easily damaged by unfairness particularly when it comes from people they have been trained to believe like parents and teachers.

Everything that you are going to put in your memoirs is hidden at this very moment in your mind. How do you get it out? Let me show you the most productive way and the way that is the most fun.

Pretend the two of us are talking.

ME: I can remember back when I was three years old, I

think. I remember having scarlet fever and thinking the bed was moving. I remember a coffee grinder attached to the wall, and once I pulled the handle and got coffee grounds in my eyes.

YOU: I can remember things from before I started school, and I was four when I started afternoon kindergarten.

ME: There were two old maid sisters living next to us. We shared a common walk to the rear of our homes. They had a collection of china figurines in their window and my sister and I used to stop and look at them.

One day one of the women came out and asked if I'd like to see one more closely. Then she put it in my hand. While I was looking at it, I dropped it. It shattered, of course.

I ran into the house, and after that I'd only use the common walkway when I had to. I'd go out the front door instead.

What strikes me odd today is that having hurt this kind woman in this way I found myself disliking her.

YOU: That's not so unusual. When I first started to drive I got a ticket for illegal parking. The fine was $8. I didn't dare tell my parents, and I didn't have that kind of money, but I was able to borrow it from a girlfriend. She had a Saturday job, and she'd saved it. The effect was rather startling. I found myself resenting the fact that she held a certain power over me because she knew my secret. I paid her back a dollar at a time, and I resented it very much. Each time after the first few times I felt that I needed the money more than she did. When I finished paying her back I felt superior to her because I'd proved that I can be trusted to meet my obligation.

ME: Did the friendship last?

YOU: No. I wound up in a different circle of girls. I guess she represented an unpleasant experience in my life, and subconsciously I suppose, I avoided her.

What we have here is a bit of idle conversation brought on by the question, "What is the first thing you remember?" That question wasn't really answered, but that's not important. What is important is that it stimulated thoughts of the past.

Now look at the subject matter. Is getting a traffic ticket

important enough to immortalize in your memoirs? Well, you've got to concede that it taught you at least two lessons, one concerning the debilitating effect of having friends do you favors, and the other concerning the parents vs. child relationship that can make children feel a bit less a part of family.

The point to be made here, however, is how easily conversation stimulates the memory and provides grist for the memoirs.

Let us say the conversation actually had taken place. Then as soon as you got the chance, you would make a brief note reading "got ticket — borrowed — resented the lender."

You would tuck this away, and at some later time write of this incident more fully. Now it may read:

I learned to drive when I was 16. You didn't have tests and drivers licenses in those days. You just drove. Mom didn't know how to drive, and she was afraid to learn, but she insisted that I learn how. Dad took me out one time, and that was that. He said if anything happened to his only daughter he'd never forgive himself and if anything happened to his $3,000 car, he'd never forgive me.

One of the boys at school taught me in his car. We'd always wind up in the park and I learned more than driving. I can't honestly say I minded until we started getting into arguments because I wanted to drive and he wanted to park.

When I told my mother that I could drive she demanded the keys from my father, and went out for a ride with me. A few days later she needed something from the store, and Dad handed me the keys. I was accepted as one of the family's drivers.

Then one day I borrowed the car to go to the library, stayed too long, and came out to find a parking ticket. I had to come up with $8 for the fine in the next five days. That was a lot of money for a high school girl. I didn't dare tell Dad. I stewed about it for three days, and finally approached Sally Kloss. She was one of my very good friends. I'd taken her for rides with me. She worked Saturdays and had money of her own. She volunteered to lend me the money, and I took it. I swore her to secrecy and paid her back a dollar a week out of my allowance.

But a strange thing happened to our relationship. After the first few payments I found myself resenting her because she knew an unpleasant secret and because I was under a burdensome obligation to her. I didn't like giving her one dollar of my limited allowance each week.

By the time I finished paying her I felt more as if I was doing her a favor than as if she'd done me one. I never liked her after that.

In my entire life I haven't been able to work out a satisfactory way of doing favors or accepting them. I think my eventual answer was to treat them as casually as possible.

What you have here is a lesson in your life, but as you think about it, you recall that eventually you did tell your parents. This will promote an anecdote plus some insight into family life.

A month after I got the traffic ticket cleared up, I told my parents about it. My father didn't seem to be nearly as upset about the ticket as he was by the fact that I didn't come to him with my problem. A child doesn't go running around for weeks with a troubled mind. She brings it to her parents and they work something out.

When he finished Mom laughed and said, "I think you did the right thing. I'd never tell your father about traffic tickets either."

Then we all laughed together, and suddenly I felt the wonderful warmth of family.

There undoubtedly are some questions. Let me ask them and answer them.

What sort of supplies do I need to write my memoirs? There's a chapter in this guide on that.

How will I ever gather enough material to justify my memoirs? There are five chapters on that.

I don't think I've ever done anything important enough to write about. Of course you have. You survived. That is one of the important accomplishments of life. Your memories will surprise you.

I'm not a writer. How do I put my thoughts in words? The same way you put that question into words, but there's a whole chapter on that.

I seem to be winding up with a hodge-podge of material. How do I organize it? There's a chapter on that.

When I finally finish my memoirs, how do I preserve them and how do I make certain they're not lost among a lot of useless things I'll be leaving behind? You guessed it. There's a chapter on that.

Think of a memoir as involving (1) something that happened, (2) the thoughts it generated, and (3) the lesson it taught you.

Your memories will come to you as you begin to share them with friends.

The questions you have in mind now will be dealt with in the remaining chapters of this guide.

II. How This Guide Came to Be Written

*This is optional reading,
but it may help you understand
why it's such a good idea
to leave memoirs, and how
unfortunate it is that your
parents didn't leave theirs.*

My daughter, Betty, picked me up at the Detroit airport. I took the wheel for the fifty-minute drive back to Toledo. I assured her that all went well on the trip, and she told me that everything was fine at home. We then settled down to our own thoughts and let time and the scenery roll by.

Eventually I became aware that she was studying my profile intently.

"Well?" I challenged. She'd been caught in the act.

She smiled sheepishly, and then asked, "Dad, how does it feel to be over sixty?"

"I really don't know," I laughed. "I've never felt over sixty."

Actually I was over sixty-five at the time, and she knew it, and I knew it, and Medicare knew it, but the evasive answer satisfied her, and she returned to the scenery and her thoughts.

Her question, however, disturbed me. It hadn't occurred to me that my children think of me as old. Although Betty and her brother, Bob, have been living away from home for years and are self-supporting, I'd always assumed that I am still the genuine practicing head of the family, the prime source of advice, information, and emergency loans, the consultant, the confidant, and the answerer of questions.

Is it possible that my children now think of me as the family elder, a kind of worn-out figurehead to which a certain amount of deference is due for old time's sake? Is our relationship held together only by the demands our culture makes upon the young to respect the old? Am I no longer the rock to their Gibraltar?

As we drove along I toyed with the idea of shocking Betty with some truths.

I still enjoy going to bed with her mother, and exercise the option at most opportunities. Her mother and I still have pet names and private games. I usually touch her when she walks by, and we often laugh with each other for the sheer fun of being together. I could tell her that.

But I soon ruled out that approach. The subject matter would be out of character, and I feared the mental images it might conjure up each time Betty saw her mother and me together.

I considered another tack. I could point out that I still have my own hair and teeth, and have missed no more than three days of work in the past forty years because of illness. I had just carried my own bags from the baggage claim area to the car with no help from her, and am now driving along at fifteen miles over the speed limit. Does that sound like a has-been?

I had to veto those arguments too. Arguing that one is well-preserved precludes recognition of one's advancing age. I didn't even want to do that at the moment.

The best answer seemed to be no answer at all. Besides, it was pretty apparent that Betty really didn't care what it was like to be over sixty. She was just finding out what it was like to be over thirty.

Nevertheless, I was left with the realization of how little our children know of the real us. As I thought about it, I could understand why. In our desire to be good living examples for them, we keep a lot of ourselves hidden. We must. We don't want them growing up like us. We want them growing up better. Come to think of it, that's rather noble.

In the days that followed it became apparent to me that it would be a good feeling to be able to make the children aware of the lives that came before their lives, the struggles their grand-parents faced in coming to this country; how by great industry and love they were able to make life much easier, and how I in turn was able to make my children's lives better.

I decided to do just that. Then I discovered I couldn't. When would I find time to tell them, and when would they find time to listen? If they listened, would they remember? If they remembered, would they pass it on? If they passed it on to their children, would their children listen, remember, and pass on? Besides, what if I were boring?

That's when the idea of writing my memoirs struck me, a record of my life's adventures, thoughts, and lessons put in writing to be read after my death by my children's children and their children and for generations to come. One could be relatively outspoken in such work. One could tell it as it was, or even as it wasn't. One would be reaching beyond the grave to exert influence on a future generation or generations. One could have a lot of fun collecting the information and contemplating its future. One could even get a feeling of power.

The same Betty and Bob who might snicker at my telling of stories of how I tried to help make the world safe for democracy in the Great War, would kill to see what I was going to tell posterity about them.

As a newsman of more than forty years' experience, a feature writer of in-depth articles and biographies, and a teacher and student of creative writing, I had a pretty good idea of procedure and technique necessary for leaving one's memoirs, but I never dreamed of the fringe benefits that would go with it.

Very early in the process I became aware of one glaring weakness. Despite the fact that we lived in the same city until their deaths, I really knew no more about my parents than my children seem to know about me.

After Dad died, Mom suffered a stroke that left her blind. She took to a wheelchair and waited for death. I visited her daily in the nursing home, and watched her world grow smaller and smaller until it consisted only of the two of us. Conversation became difficult. She asked no questions, and her answers to mine were brief. We spent a great deal of time sitting together in silence. It was depressing, and I felt guilty because I found myself dreading these daily visits and cutting them shorter and shorter.

It was after I'd started collecting my memoirs that I felt a need to account for how the family got to Toledo, Ohio. I didn't know. Mom would know, but could she tell me in her present state? Despite the fact that she wasn't very responsive, I was going to ask. I was going to work very hard to get some answers. I would ask and ask and press and press. It would be a game to see how much I could learn about Mother's life from her.

I started by asking about her childhood in Hungary. Her memories were vague and her answers were brief. She couldn't remember names or places, and even when I'd mention the names of cities and rivers in Hungary that I'd gleaned from an old atlas, she didn't seem to be much interested.

I worked my way through her education, her parents' decision to send her to America alone at the age of 14, her arrival at Ellis Island, and her meeting with relatives here. None of these sparked her interest, although she recalled with some emotion her father running after the train that was to take her to the ship to America, and shouting something to her.

Then one day I hit the jackpot. I mentioned her wedding. The life she remembered seemed to start with the day it became obvious that she and Dad would be married. She spoke of this period in detail, needing only an occasional question to prime her. Even if my memoirs are never to be completed, the contribution it made in reawakening her mind for a few weeks would be reward enough.

I knew that Dad also had come to America from Hungary. He was 15, and had no family waiting at the boat. His father had given him a bit of money and the word that Hungary was no place to live anymore. He set off with two friends his age for Bremen, Germany, and passage to America. It must have been a fearsome experience, but a lot of young people were doing it. What amounted to an underground railroad had been set up, and the youngsters found guides to take them across borders and around towns until they arrived safely at the port.

The interviews with Mom proved to be a fine example of how much meaty information there is in the commonplace, how much one can deduce from a relatively ordinary life, how ordinary stories take on extraordinary meaning when they are close to home.

"It was a small wedding," Mom told me, "but it was very nice. Everybody was poor then, but Aunt Kate fixed the tenement up so beautifully that I couldn't believe it."

Mom lived with Aunt Kate. Dad lived with cousins in another tenement in the same building.

"Practically the only people there were relatives, but we had plenty of food and wine and a beautiful cake. I remember there were musicians and dancing. Your father loved to dance. (I never suspected that.) We danced in the halls and on the stairways, and even neighbors joined in."

"Where did you go for a honeymoon?" I asked.

Mom laughed. I don't remember the last time she'd laughed before that.

"Who could afford a honeymoon?" she smiled. "In our class we read about honeymoons in books, we didn't take them. We'd found a tenement on Seventh Avenue and Avenue C, and I could hardly wait to get into it—my very own apartment.

"For weeks before the wedding we'd been going to used furniture stores and auctions picking out pieces. Your father had a cousin who was very good at bidding. We'd go together. I'd find something I liked, and she'd negotiate for it. Do you remember the dining room chairs carved with figures of Dutch skaters? That was a wedding present from your father's uncle. He bought them at a used furniture store."

"Didn't it bother you to start out with used furniture?" I asked. Mom laughed again.

"In those days sleeping three in a bed and six in a room didn't bother us. Why should used furniture?

"We didn't live in comfort a lot in those days, but we helped each other get along. We shared everything including troubles. In this new country of ours, we lived with the thought that tomorrow would be better. The idea was to survive until the right tomorrow came along."

My mother, the philosopher!

Then we talked about the store. The folks opened a small dry goods store in which they manufactured house dresses and aprons for the wholesale and retail trade. It was attached to the house. It also was attached to our lives.

Dad worked at a salaried job during the day and made patterns and cut material for the store at night. He professed to hate the store, and considered it Mom's. Yet, the store made it possible for the family to survive the Depression and be generous and helpful to friends and relatives.

At one session I asked Mom how she and Dad happened to open the store, in view of his dislike for it. I'd always thought Dad got his way around our house. The answer opened my eyes.

When Mom arrived in New York, she related, she was sent as a day worker to an American family. (My mother, a servant?!) She was expected to clean and help with the cooking and baking. Actually she was too small for such strenuous work, but she was a fine seamstress and constantly found things to mend. The woman of the house was so pleased with her work that she kept her on to sew and do dishes, and left the heavy work to others.

Eventually my parents joined relatives in Toledo. Dad planned to go into a new laundry business. Mom was raising two of us then, but she still found time to sew and mend for a sister-in-law.

One day a neighbor-friend asked Mom how much she charged for sewing. Mom quickly explained that she didn't charge anything. How could one charge a relative for sewing?

"Then don't sew for relatives," the friend advised. "Sew for me. I can get you all the work you can handle. As long as you sew, you may as well get paid."

When Dad found out that Mom was sewing for the neighbors he got pretty upset and ordered her to stop. This was a noble thing to do, but the truth of the matter was that the laundry was failing, and the folks needed the money. Mom continued to sew, but she did it secretly.

The laundry didn't work out, and Dad wanted to move back to New York. Mom absolutely refused. It was no place to raise children, she argued. There was plenty of work in Toledo. If Dad returned he would return alone.

Dad stayed. As far as I know it was the first and only major revolt that Mom ever staged.

One day a friend of Dad's managed to convince him that the way to get along in this country was to go into business for yourself. Mom was all for it. Dad didn't like the idea. Then one day the friend dragged Dad out to see a house with store attached, available at a price that was difficult to refuse. Dad gave in. Mom's sewing came out of the closet. The roots were beginning to take.

It may not be much as great lives go, but in my memoirs it will explain to the progeny how the family got its start in Toledo, Ohio.

Both Mom and Dad are dead now, of course. They left me with deep regrets that I don't know more about them as human beings and a desire to make certain that my children will know more about the kind of person I am, or at least the kind I want them to think I am.

I think that once I learned the story of my parents' each leaving their families at a very young age to seek out a new life in a new land it gave me personal courage to do whatever had to be done and to face whatever is to come. I could be brave now that I knew courage runs in the family.

As I thought about the task of passing the story of my life on to future generations it quickly became evident that an autobiography would be difficult. It would require detailed research and organization, and much of it would really not be worth recording. It would be tedious. Even if I started it, I probably would never finish it.

That's when the idea of memoirs occurred to me. These required no research, could be written in short takes, and organizing them in some kind of final form would require only paper shuffling.

It wasn't even the lonely job I thought it would be. It gave me an excuse to talk with others about my past. In groups we traded stories, ideas, and opinions. Maybe we even traded lies.

Now, as my notes pile up around me, I relish the thought that someday my grandchildren will be reading them — and the things they are going to find out about their parents, well, it is just a little bit short of blackmail.

III. Memoir Clubs and Classes

*Herein are contained a few
notes on the technical and
social advantages of gathering
in small groups for pursuing
the hobby of memoir-
collecting along with a
suggested procedure.*

The process of collecting your memoirs should be a very social one. While we like to consider our thoughts private, they really aren't. As a matter of truth, if we don't have someone to share them with they're hardly worth having.

It should also be noted that our thoughts are sharpest when honed on the opinions of others. In other words, the more you talk things over with others the clearer you will be on your thoughts.

Actually, you need other people to help you collect your memoirs even though they may know nothing about you.

Think of it this way. Unless you are famous, little of your life has been preserved in books, news reports, letters, magazines or other written or printed forms.

You must draw your life's stories mainly from your memories. You do this by talking with others—friends, strangers, anyone who will listen. It sounds crazy, but as pointed out elsewhere in this guide, your hobby of memoir-collecting is your excuse for starting conversations with strangers and talking about yourself. Talking about yourself opens your memory. Exchanging memories and experiences with others reminds you of things long forgotten.

The easiest place to discuss your memories openly is at a club or in a class organized for the specific purpose of helping its members collect and organize their memoirs. As each discusses an experience of his own, others are reminded of experiences in the same field.

All it takes is five or six people, and if you find any hesitancy in talking about personal thoughts you start out with a nice general question.

Where were you and what did you think when the Japanese attacked Pearl Harbor?

What was your reaction when you learned of the existence of the atomic bomb?

How did the assassination of President Kennedy affect you emotionally?

What did you think when you saw live television pictures of the astronauts stepping onto the surface of the moon?

These are rather impersonal and safe questions. Yet any one of them could get a roomful of people talking about their reactions and themselves. In that atmosphere it is a simple matter to switch to mutual closer-to-home experiences — becoming parents, experiencing death, marriage, leaving home and on, and on and on.

People involved in memoir clubs or classes are more likely to see their writing projects through to a finish. The pleasure of attending and participating in the sessions is a moving force for most of us. Without it we are more likely to procrastinate and eventually give up.

The difference between a memoir class and a memoir club is the nature of the leadership. In the former a teacher moves the class through the steps described in the guide, checking to make certain that everything is understood by everyone, and giving individual attention to those needing additional help.

In the club it is more a matter of learning by comparison with members who feel that they've succeeded in getting the desired results in any one phase, and discussing with the others how they arrived at their conclusions, using their work as examples.

In either case, to keep the program moving forward it may be desirable to set up a schedule to keep the work moving forward. A typical schedule:

First session. Start out with a question that will create an exchange of thoughts and information.

What is the greatest lesson you learned from experience?

If you were hungry and could find no one to give you work, would you beg or would you steal?

At what age were you the most attractive to the other sex?

It is very likely that in a short time you will have members speaking in the first person about their thoughts, their beliefs, and their experiences. You now call the group to order again and explain that this is the sort of thing that will be happening in future sessions.

Next (and refer to Chapter IV), discuss the supplies and equipment. Also spend a little time talking about note taking, writing just enough words about a memory to make certain that later when you want to write the memory in full the note will serve as a reminder.

Second session. Discuss Chapter V which deals generally with unlocking one's memories, and then get the members started on collecting dates. Once they understand how and why this is done, turn the discussion to memories inspired by the dates. The list of dates may be completed in private.

Stress the criteria for determining if a memoir is worth inclusion.

Third session. Deal with Chapters VI, VII, and VIII, talking about the three basic forms of memoirs, the facts of one's life, the thoughts that life generated, and the lessons it taught.

The accent here should be on letting the members exchange memories so that they stimulate each other. It may be well to suggest that anyone who has started getting his memoirs down on paper is welcome to read them for discussion and criticism.

Fourth session. Discuss Chapter X — briefly if none of the members feel that they have a great event to include in the memoirs, and, of course, in more detail if interest is shown.

Leave time for the all-important exchange of memoirs.

Fifth session. Refer to Chapter XI and get into the project of helping members pick an imaginary reader for whom each is pretending to write his memoirs. Then switch to the problem of determining what kind of image of himself the writer would like to convey to his future readers. Finally, work on the thrust of the message that each feels he wants his work to carry.

Sixth session. This is the time to think about the beginning and the ending of the memoirs. Explain how the work must begin with a statement of who the writer is and the circumstances under which he is writing this. It should include the place, the date, the age, the writer's health, and any special situation that exists at the time of the writing. It may also contain a general statement of the writer's view of his own life.

The closing paragraphs of the autobiography should be a farewell address to the reader, possibly a hope that the world is a better place in which to live, a hope that the reader has found what he has read here helpful and interesting, maybe a final comment on some philosophy of life. Chapters XI and XII will help.

Seventh session. This session should deal with sorting out the notes that have been collected, putting them in related piles, and then creating an outline to be followed in the final manuscript as described in Chapter XII.

Eighth session. Ask members to read samples of their writing, and exchange comments on them. Stress simplicity. Stress the fact that getting the message across is the one and only requirement. Do what must be done to instill confidence into the writers.

Come prepared to discuss the local availability and costs of such items as copy machine services and typing services for those who may be willing to invest in additional or more readable manuscripts.

Determine if there is a depository for local history in your area, and if it would be interested in acquiring copies of these personal histories.

Demonstrate the use of the self-adhesive photo album as a method of assuring permanency to these historic pages.

If your classes generate more enthusiasm than you can handle comfortably, it may be an idea after the basic lecture in each session to divide the class up in groups of six or so in order that each member will have a great opportunity to discuss his work with others. Your role then is moving from group to group and making yourself available for questions and explanations.

Using the Memoirs in This Guide

Scattered throughout this guide are a large number of samples of memoirs (indented a little from the left). If things bog down, read several of them aloud and see if anyone in the group has comment, similar memoirs, or opposing memoirs.

You may also want to challenge the members' memories by using the list of words offered in Chapter XIV.

Review. The easiest way to remember the things that went on in your life is to talk about them to anyone who will listen.

Your memoir-collecting gives you a reason to talk about yourself. Take advantage of it. Try listening also. The things you hear will inspire you.

Working in a group is much preferred, but whether you work with several people or undertake writing your memoirs by yourself, this book will provide all the help you need.

In preparing your memoirs there is one infallible way to determine whether you are doing it correctly: If you enjoy what you're doing, then you are doing it right.

A Note About Notes

A good part of your research will consist of making brief notes on scraps of paper.

When you are taking information from books and documents, the notes necessarily must be reasonably complete. Most of your note-taking, however, will come as you are speaking with people or prodding your memory privately.

Notes need be just complete enough so that when the time comes to elaborate on them for your final manuscript you will remember of what they are supposed to remind you. Yet they should be brief enough so that your writing them does not disrupt the flow of the conversation.

Many professional interviewers do not take notes until the interview is almost over. Then they will recall the points they care to record and ask the subject about them again. This time they will make fairly complete notes.

There are several reasons for this.

For one thing most interviewers generally are interested in creating an informal and relaxed atmosphere in which the interview actually can be turned into a friendly two-way conversation. This cannot be achieved if the subject is going to be kept conscious of the fact that this is an interview and not merely small talk, and he is going to be very conscious of this if the questioner sits there with pencil poised on pad ready to write.

In any interview, when the scribbling starts, the subject begins to ask himself "What did I say? Why is he writing it down? Why didn't he write down the thing I said before? Am I talking too much? What is he trying to get me to say?" Goodbye, flowing conversation.

The best technique is to take as few notes as possible. After the conversation is over, recreate what was said in your mind and make your notes.

In groups, where your note taking isn't likely to be so distracting, make very brief notes during the conversation, and elaborate on them as soon afterward as possible.

IV. Paper, Pen and a Self-Adhesive Photo Album

*This chapter deals largely
with the material you will need
to make your memoirs live
practically for ever and ever.*

The one distinctive piece of equipment that you will require in the pursuit of collecting your memoirs is a magnetic self-adhesive photo album. These are generally available in department stores and discount houses, and frequently are offered at reduced prices.

The album pages are of heavy card stock and lined with an adhesive that makes paper stick and yet permits it to be removed without tearing or damaging. Each page also comes with a transparent vinyl sheet which will cover your writings and protect them from the ravages of atmosphere and time for years and probably centuries.

The pages are bound together with spiral bindings or looseleaf rings and are firm enough to stand up under much turning. The albums come in atttractive heavy covers and may be stored in bookcases where they will remain out of the way, yet easily available. It is advised that you buy the 100-page album.

You may also find a word book a necessity. A word book is a relatively inexpensive paperback that lists words alphabetically, and is used to check spelling and hyphenation. It is much faster and easier to use than the conventional dictionary. You won't need a dictionary, of course. These are your memoirs, and you won't be using words you don't understand.

Except for the album and word book, the other supplies are commonplace and easily available. For starters, any kind of writing instruments and any kind of paper is satisfactory. Eventually, for the final draft, you may want a pretty good grade of paper. After all, you expect it to be kept around for a long, long time.

There are many ways to proceed, but for starters let us recommend the simple device of collecting brief notes to be expanded into memoirs as time permits. To store the notes you use five business envelopes labeled *dates, history, thoughts, lessons,* and *miscellany*.

A useful although not vital bit of information in prodding your memory is the date. It may be a good idea to collect them. Just as a starting point you may want to record all the dates you can remember. Births, deaths, years in school, years of employment, anniversaries, and on and on. You will find these extremely helpful in organizing your memoirs in the final draft. Keep your dates together in the envelope labeled *dates*.

In the *history* envelope you will store those notes that have to do with the events in your life, the things that actually happened. In my envelope I have a note which reads "Night wife was born. Mae. Storm." In its final form it will read:

> Heavy winds and rain pelted the city the night that my wife was born. Wires were down, streets were flooded, and the fear instilled by the stormy trip to the hospital was second only to the fear that the car may not get there in time.
>
> The hospital itself was a comparatively small wooden building. It had once been a private home. Wings were added here and there, but it was a good thirty years behind being modern.
>
> They were still timing labor pains when the storm cut the hospital powerlines. There was no emergency generator.
>
> Thunder rattled the building, and lightning danced at the windows and suddenly there was a child. It was as if the baby came not from the womb but from the storm. The mother told the doctor the baby would be named Storm.
>
> When the new mother awoke again, the terror of the night had passed. The sun was bright, the air was fresh, the

whole city seemed to be washed clean. The mother held the tiny, pink, sweet-smelling infant, and named her Mae instead, after her favorite month.

This is an event of importance in my life and in the life of my progeny. Will it be included in the final draft of my memoirs? That is a decision to be made later, but there is no doubt in my mind that it will be. After all, somewhere along the line some children will be named after their grandmother or great grandmother. They ought to know how the name came into the family.

Now what is the nature of the notes to be stored in the *thoughts* envelope? These generally are means of expressing the philosophy you've developed about life. We are not necessarily talking about great, deep, heavy thoughts. Your lightest opinions also help tell the kind of person you are—or possibly when they are being read by your great grandchildren—were. (As I write my memoirs I find myself trying to charm its readers. I think I want to make them wish I were still around.)

As an example of *thoughts* let me cite from a conversation that arose at a meeting of memoir-writers. Just to get this group of five women talking, I asked the question: "If someone were to tell you that you could keep either your telephone or your television set, but that you would have to give one or the other up, what would you do?"

Mrs. Marks: If someone gave me such a choice, I'd kill him. I need them both. My television set was stolen once, and it was three days before I replaced it. During that time I felt like I couldn't breathe.

Mrs. Epps: I don't know if my telephone is such a big deal. If it weren't for the phone maybe the kids would come over and see me instead of just calling me up.

What I do now is call them up and pretend I'm having trouble breathing. Then they come.

Mrs. Marks: Don't they get mad when they see you fooled them?

Mrs. Epps: I tell them it was a mistake. I was making obscene phone calls and I dialed them by mistake. But which would they rather have, a mother who does obscene breathing on the telephone or a mother who is dying of asthma? They get the message.

What kind of memoirs are these, you may ask. Mrs. Marks is telling her readers of the dependence of her generation on these instruments of communication. It also indicates a certain amount of loneliness.

In the case of Mrs. Epps, we can tell from her story that she is a peppery, independent, outspoken individual, with a proprietary kind of love of family. I don't know that I'd like to have her for a mother, but if she were my grandmother I'd take pride and pleasure in telling this story of hers to my friends.

The notes to make certain that the stories aren't forgotten could be very simple. For Mrs. Marks, "television" and "breathing" and for Mrs. Epps, "obscene breathing or dying of asthma" should do.

Now let us consider the nature of notes that would be deposited in the *lessons* envelope. I have one that reads "sleeping warm in World War II." In my memoirs it will read something like this:

The world doesn't seem to have learned much from World War II, but I did. I learned to sleep warm, work hard, and try not to think about it.

I would be lying if I said that I wasn't frightened during my time in military service. I would also be lying if I said that I truly had something to be frightened of. While the potential for disaster was ever present, I experienced neither near disaster nor disaster.

I was older than most men around me in service and less physical. I wasn't always certain that I would be able to do what was expected of me. I couldn't adopt a live, laugh and be happy for tomorrow we die attitude because I didn't want to die tomorrow. I had a wife and a life I hoped to come back to.

One night during training I drew guard duty. It didn't amount to anything. There were three one-hour tours of walking a post with two hours for sleep in the guard hut between each shift.

I was just getting ready to sack out when a soldier sitting on the edge of a bunk next to mine and smoking a cigarette said to no one in particular, "This crap is worse than KP." KP is kitchen police, which is a full day of doing the dirty work for the cooks and bakers, cleaning up mess halls, and moving a lot of garbage.

"I'll take guard duty every time," I answered. "I'm up almost this much just going to the can."

"I hate it," he said. "It gives a man too much time to think." He was right about that.

"The worst thing about the service is thinking," he went on, "thinking about what's going to happen, thinking about the people back home, wondering whether you're ever going to be a civilian again. And the worst time for thinking is during the night.

"They roust you so early for KP, and they work you so hard that you don't have time to think during the day, and you're too tired and too busy sleeping to think at night."

He was absolutely right. If you could keep from thinking too much about what might happen, then life wouldn't be too bad. At least in our war, World War II, we knew why we were fighting, and that we'd have to keep at it until it was over. Thinking about it wouldn't help. It could only hurt.

After that I made it my personal goal to sleep warm and comfortable. On bivouac, on the transport, wherever I was I made it my business to make up a sack that would be warm and comfortable. I also carried a book and a flashlight so that if I couldn't sleep I would read instead of think.

I carried this ability to stop thinking back to my civilian life. If you can do something about it, do it. If you can't, don't think about it.

I'll admit that I can't apply this easily to affairs involving the wife and kids. I worry about them whenever the opportunity presents itself, but beyond that I've avoided a lot of stress with the policy, "Don't stay awake worrying about your adversaries. Let them lose sleep worrying about you."

The envelope *Miscellany* is meant to receive notes that don't seem to fit in the other categories yet is the sort of thing you might want to pass on for its entertainment value.

I can't say that I liked practical jokes, but I must admit that I sometimes enjoyed creative practical jokers.

Back in the days when one could park an automobile at a meter for five cents, I met a man whose hobby was putting nickels in the meters that already had been ticketed for parking overtime.

After inserting the coin he'd walk off tickled by the thought of how the owner would react when he found his car had been ticketed despite the fact that the meter still showed parking time left.

We will deal more with sources of inspiration for your memoirs and how to organize them later in the text. Meanwhile you can start collecting notes for the envelopes.

Eventually you will need a reasonably good grade of typing or writing paper for your finished product, but for the time being you can get by with whatever is available.

The only thing left to be said on the subject was said by a very wise journalism instructor who told our class, "You people are more than bright enough to learn everything I have to teach you. There is only one way you can flunk this course. Let me catch you anywhere and anytime without a ready pencil and sheet of paper and it is an automatic flunk. A reporter who is not ready to take notes at any time is not a reporter."

The same thing goes for memoir-writers.

Review. The following equipment and supply are recommended for pursuing the hobby of collecting your memoirs:

A 100-page self-adhesive photo album; a word book to assist in spelling; writing instruments; paper; envelopes labeled: *dates, history, thoughts, lessons,* and *miscellany.*

V. Unlocking Your Memories

This is the most important chapter. The stories of your life are locked in your memory, and getting them out may alter your life style. Suddenly you have an excuse, a need and a reason to talk about yourself to anyone willing to listen.

The story of your life is locked in your memory, and the immediate problem is to find the key.

At least, that's the way it is with most of us. The mind is willing, but the memory is weak. We're going to have to force the lock a bit.

Don't feel too bad about it. That can be the best part of the whole project—getting help in recalling.

Before we get too deeply into the devices for helping memory let us consider what we are seeking for our memoirs. What do we preserve and what shall we let ourselves forget again?

To make this decision we use certain criteria: (1) Is the event important in your life? (2) Did it stimulate thought or teach you a lesson worth passing on? (3) Does it make good reading?

If the answer to any of these questions is yes, the event and all the story that surrounds it deserves serious consideration for inclusion in your memoirs. Make a note of it, and stick it into the proper envelope. If you have doubts, give the benefit to the note. You can always eliminate it in the final compilation.

Let us consider a hypothetical case:

You played ball in a church softball league, and hit a
home run with bases loaded that won the championship for
your team.

Based on the criteria above, it appears that you struck out. In
terms of history it just doesn't qualify. Unless it did something more
than make you the hero for a brief moment, it really isn't worth
recording for posterity. Right? Maybe not.

Maybe you learned something from the experience. Let the
memory run.

You recall that you prayed for a home run before you
came to bat.

Now maybe you've got a point on the power of prayer. You
may have some very definite opinions on that matter, and in the
name of honesty you must point out something else.

You always prayed that you'd get a home run, but this is
the only time you actually hit one.

The greatest stimulant to sharpening memory and aiding recall
is conversation—trading stories with friends, relatives and even
strangers. It can be a life style-changing joy. Repeat that. It is the
most important single point in this entire book. It may well be the
whole project's greatest reward. It gives you a legitimate reason to
talk to people, and you will be talking about a subject on which you
are a true authority—yourself.

All it takes is enough nerve to make an initial approach. Once
you learn how easy it is you'll never again be lonely among
people.

Let us spend some time considering this aspect of your
research.

We will start right off with the boldest and most difficult approach to research-by-conversation—talking to strangers. If you
master this, you may enjoy it so much, you'll have to discipline
yourself to find time for writing. You are going to try to open a conversation with a stranger and get him talking about himself. You

will respond by talking about yourself, and in the course of the exchange he will remind you of things about yourself long forgotten.

Professional interviewers do this sort of thing very well. They reduce the interview to a friendly give-and-take conversation, putting the subject at ease and making him willing to talk. They have a legitimate reason to talk to their subjects. You need an excuse.

Your excuse is that you are collecting your memoirs and it helps your thinking to talk about it with other people. Most people are happy to help other people think, and they are flattered by the invitation.

Let us imagine such an approach: You are sitting next to a stranger in a bus.

"Pardon me. This may sound silly to you, but I'm writing an autobiography and I need some help in sorting out my thinking. Would you mind if we talked a bit?"

"Well, as long as you're not selling anything I guess it would be all right."

He's puzzled and suspicious, but he'll soon get over it. Don't lose your nerve.

"I'm trying to think of a way to express a lesson which I'd like to pass on to my grandchildren through my memoirs. It goes, 'The easier things are, the harder life gets.' Does that make sense to you?"

It probably doesn't, so you go on.

"The big crises in my life were the Depression, World War II, and one serious illness. During these times everyone was close. We understood problems. We tried to help. We worked together. We knew what we were doing on earth. We knew what had to be done.

"When things got good, though, we didn't need each other. Each of us had all we needed for the creature comforts, and we went our separate ways. It's like security brings on loneliness. When someone needs your help you are an angel. When the same person no longer needs help you are a busybody. Is that how life is?

"When I'm sick, my children are right there ready to help me. When I'm well, though, I'm lucky if I see them every two or three weeks. Given sickness or health, there are times when I think I'd pick sickness."

"Maybe you're right," the stranger offers. "We never had much money during the Depression, but somehow we never went hungry. I marvel at my parents for the way they got us through those times."

"That's my point," you agree. "You appreciate your parents because they were tested by the Depression. But what tested you when you were raising your children? You might have sent your children to college, bought them cars, but because times were pretty good, could they appreciate it? They probably thought of it as their fair share of the family income, period.

"I worked in a factory during the war. It seems like all of us knew whose husband was in service and where he was serving, and how often he wrote, and what he said in the letters. There were a bunch of us, but we couldn't be closer if we were sisters, and yet most of them were the type of people I'd be very unlikely to know except for the war."

Replies the stranger, "My father used to say, if you want a man to remember you, get him to do you a favor. I think he's absolutely right. We remember favors we do others longer than the favors they do us."

And on and on.

Now, what have you gained by this conversation, as far as memoirs are concerned?

You've solidified your thinking on the good things about bad times, and you picked up some potential material on the power of having favors done for you.

Your children don't write often enough? You can write and tell them to write oftener and maybe they will—once. More effectively you can write and tell them that you lost Cousin Mae's address, and you need it right away. Which is likely to get the most positive results?

Pass that on to your progeny.

Let us imagine a conversation with your friends. They already know about your memoirs. Maybe they're even a bit sick of it. Among friends, though, you can be more personal and more controversial, and that gives you much more latitude for getting something going. Let's try a bit of shock and controversy.

"I remember my daughter used to use that stock line on me, 'I didn't ask to be born!'" you begin.

"Mine used to say that, too," your friend might say.

"I finally got sick of it and found a way to stop her. 'Of course you asked to be born,' I told her. 'There were 5,000 sperms trying to get to my egg, and you were the one that made it. Don't tell me you didn't push a lot of other sperms out of the way to get there first, and don't tell me you didn't want to be born.'

"She was so shocked that a mother should think about a daughter that way that she never used that line again."

Now comes the reply, "I used to hate it when my daughter would say that. Now I hope she does, I'll give her your answer.

"Of course, she's married now, and has two beautiful children. She says they drive her crazy, but I love them. I call them my avengers. 'They are getting even for me for all the trouble you caused me,' I tell her. We laugh a lot about it, but I think I mean it."

"I might borrow that thought for my memoirs," you reply. "Our grandchildren give us the love that we hoped to get from our children, and they provide also the punishment for our children that they so richly deserved, but we never gave them. No wonder we're so crazy about our grandchildren."

This now has led you into the field of children and punishment.

"What is the severest punishment you ever inflicted on your children?" you ask.

It is a legitimate question, and what is more, you are prepared to provide your own answer.

"The cruellest thing I ever did to my daughter, I think, is something that I said. It also was the cruellest thing I ever did to myself. She was moping about her dull and dismal life—what she really needed was a boyfriend—and I was thinking about how it wouldn't hurt if she moped up in her room (which she could also mop up while she was there).

"Anyhow, I was tired of putting up with this sullenness, and one day I blurted out, 'The only reason that you were born is that your father couldn't find an abortionist that he considered safe for me.' What a horrible thing to say to a growing girl!

"She ran up to her room in tears, and I followed her also in tears. What a cry we had! I think I finally convinced her that it wasn't true by saying that in those days we didn't even know about abortionists, and that she was planned just like all our other children. This is true, but God did the planning. We didn't.

"Some time later we were driving someplace and she asked her Dad whether he'd tried to have her aborted before she was born. I almost died. He just laughed. But if he'd taken the question seriously, and asked where she ever got such idea, he'd have been terribly angry with me."

From the friend comes the answer, "I always left the punishing up to my husband. He really was very wise about it. With him punishment was a deliberate thing, planned to meet each particular situation.

"I'll never forget. Once Bernie slapped his sister, and when my husband came home I told him about it. Without hesitation, he slapped Bernie right in the face, not hard but hard enough.

"'That's pain,' he told Bernie. 'That's what your sister felt when you hit her. Maybe you should feel it one more time so you understand what you did to her.' Then he hit Bernie again, and that was the end of that.

"His punishments were very interesting. Once the kids were being pretty noisy and I wasn't feeling well. I couldn't quiet them down, so, again, Herman came home from work and I complained a little.

"He looked at the children, and said, 'I understand you haven't been very considerate of your mother today. Well, the hell with you.'

"For the rest of the evening he did all the things he usually did for them, but with absolutely no sign of love or interest. At bedtime they both apologized to him, and he explained that they should be apologizing to me instead, but it ended with a lot of love.

"When the kids grew up we used to laugh about his punishments. They thought we should have called him Judge Herman, but I said we should have called him King Solomon. He was very flattered."

In this brief conversation, started by your sperm story, what have you generated? You have recalled the painful "abortion" incident as a lesson to you; you have developed an interesting idea as to the role of grandchildren in our lives, and you have some very interesting things to pass on about punishment.

This time, let us consider for a moment what autobiographical conversational research can do for the invalid or the shut-in.

The nice woman from Meals-on-Wheels comes in.

"How are we today?" she asks. That's the start of a conversation that has nowhere to go. You lie about how you feel. She lies about how she feels about how you feel, and then she leaves.

But suppose you are working on your memoirs, and she knows you are working on it, watch the difference.

"How's your book coming?" she asks, and that opens the door for you to speak about anything you have on your mind. Let's go on.

"I'm into handicaps," you reply. "I don't like being handicapped one bit, but I'm wondering if it doesn't provide me with a certain amount of comfort and security. I want to try to explain this in my book.

"Nothing is ever really expected of me, and that's bad, but it saves me from having to cope in the real world. I know what I have here, and I know I can't expect to get any more. Yet, I also am reasonably certain that I'm not likely to be called upon to do with less. I suppose there's a kind of security in being handicapped. I'm mixed up in my true feelings about my life. As soon as I can get un-mixed, I'll write about it."

The Meals-on-Wheels person spends her days with handicapped people, probably has her own ideas on the subject, and possibly she'll even welcome the chance to bring back the opinions of other handicapped types. It should open up the world for you a bit and brighten the minutes you spend with her.

The next day she is back, and sure enough, she has some ideas on the subject. Using your memoir hobby as an excuse, she asked others what they thought about being handicapped.

"None seemed to agree with you," Meals-on-Wheels reports, "but then they haven't given it the thought you did. One of the girls said there's a lot more security in two good legs and a husband than in being hidden away from society. She said she'd like to talk to you. I took her phone number."

Aha, your world grows larger. Who knows? She may start collecting memoirs also.

The deeper you get into your memoirs, the more material you will have for opening up and maintaining conversations.

Here are a few conversation openers that may help stimulate thought, argument, or anything else necessary to keep people interested and talking.

Remember, the reply you receive isn't important, it is the engaging in conversation that is.

- What is your very first awareness of life — the very first thing you can remember?
- If you didn't know how old you were, how old would you think you are?
- If you were the boss would you pay yourself as much as you are getting now?
- If you were an employer would you hire a man who steals to feed his family ahead of a man who goes on welfare to feed his family?
- When a person goes on Social Security, the government should issue him a suicide pill. If he finds he can't live happily on Social Security, he should be allowed to take the pill. What do you think of that idea?
- Time passes quickly when you are having fun or slowly when you are bored. In a perfect world it would be the other way around. That's why I don't believe God made the world. (That should get an argument started.)
- If you had a choice of being reincarnated or staying permanently dead would you take a chance on coming back and being something entirely different from what you are now?

Maybe these openers won't get them talking to you, but it certainly will get them talking about you. Actually, it's good training. Once you get used to sharing your mind with people, you'll have no trouble sharing it with your progeny.

Let us now deal with the business of retaining all the material gathered in conversation.

Nothing can derail a train of thought like someone producing paper and pencil and starting to write. Suddenly everyone becomes self-conscious and careful of what he says. So what is the answer? How do you preserve all the little gems you are gathering without destroying the exchange of discussion? Well, at best the answer isn't very good. Yet it seems to be the best way out.

Wait until a good logical break, and then announce that this is too good, you've really got to make some notes. You recall out loud a couple of the items you'd like to preserve, and immediately you'll find that you have a committee of the whole helping you with your notes, recalling things for you.

The way most of us picture notes is on 3 × 5 cards with heading and filing information and a listing of when, where, and by whom. In real life, however, notes are made on napkins, white space in newspaper ads, backs of business cards, and unpaid traffic tickets. Do it that way. It's less terrifying to the subjects.

Lincoln reportedly wrote the whole Gettysburg address on the back of an old envelope, but it couldn't have turned out better if he'd written it on parchment with a quill pen. The trick is to go through your pockets, your wallet, your purse every once in a while, gather the scraps of notes, and copy them more fully on pieces of tablet paper which you promptly deposit in the proper envelope in your file.

At this point the most promising symptom of a good set of memoirs is fat envelope files.

There are other ways for reminding, but they aren't as much fun as talking. If you have them around, however, they probably will help make your memoirs more accurate. They are:

The Family Bible	Genealogies
Letters	Photos
Scrapbooks	Newspaper Clippings
Yearbooks	Business Papers
Diaries	Souvenirs and Programs
Old City Directories	

Probably the only thing that need be said about these sources is that you may want to preserve copies of some of the items in your memoir notebook. Good clear copies may be made very reasonably on public copy machines located in most public libraries. Consider making several copies of each just in the event that you plan to make more than one copy of your memoirs.

Review. Memories are where you find them, and the easiest place to find them is in exchanging them with others.

Never rely on your recall to remember an incident. Jot down a note or two, just enough to bring it back to you when the time comes to write about it.

Other sources for information are family bibles, genealogies, letters, photos, scrapbooks, newspaper clippings, yearbooks, business papers, diaries, souvenir programs, and old city directories.

Remember the criteria for determining whether a thought or memory will be useful: Is it an event important in your life? Did it stimulate a thought or teach a lesson worth passing on? Does it make good reading?

Any one of these three reasons is good enough to make it worth including in your memoirs.

VI. Unlocking Your Memories — Collecting the Dates

*This chapter demonstrates
the use of dates as a way
of unlocking memories that
may be worth including in
your memoirs. The dates later
will be very useful in
organizing the final draft.*

Dates, God bless them. What wonderful things they are! They are so positive, so consistent, so orderly. In a life filled with uncertainty and change, nothing is as dependable as dates.

If you were born on April 12, 1920, you were 66 years old on April 12, 1986. Maybe you didn't admit to 66; maybe you didn't feel like 66; maybe you couldn't believe that you were 66, but thanks to the reliability and insistence of dates you cannot deny the arithmetic of the matter. You resigned yourself to being 66.

I rhapsodize thus on dates because they will anchor the many stories in your life where they belong, and will serve as reminders of the days gone by, and the source of many memoirs.

We cannot hope to collect facts of our lives in perfect chronological order. We must take them when and where we find them. If we can later assign dates, it will help organize the final draft.

As we rack our brains for dates, memories come pouring in. Grab them while they're hot. Make a note on each item. The note should be just detailed enough to return that item to your memory in full when the time comes to record it in your memoirs.

Let us start working on dates by taking several sheets of paper and assigning one of the following labels to each.

- Dates Concerning Forebears
- Birthdates of the Immediate Family
- Residences
- Education
- Employment
- Good Times and Bad

Now start listing all the dates you can think of and placing them on the proper sheets. If you don't have exact dates, use approximate dates. If you can't even approximate the date, list the event. Sooner or later you will be able to associate the event with an approximate date. Something else that you will remember will help determine where it fits into the chronological scheme of things.

Deposit the sheets in the envelope marked *Dates* and as new dates come to mind, add them to the proper sheet.

Let us look at examples of how dates may fit and how they may be used.

Dates Concerning Forebears

April 8, 1885	Father born in Hungary
Dec. 21, 1888	Mother born in Hungary
Summer 1900	Father escapes to U.S.
Summer 1903	Mother sent to U.S.
May 18, 1908	Parents wed in New York

Obviously not much information on the genealogy is available here, but in trying to provide all possible information for that generation of the future one may settle for a note like this:

I didn't know any of my grandparents. They never came to the United States. My Dad told me that my grandfather was a horse trader, which was the equivalent of a used car salesman. He'd buy and sell horses at the town markets.

He'd pick up a horse, bring him out to the farm, fatten him up, clean him up, and then take him back to market to sell again. Sometimes he could improve a horse by changing the way it was shod.

Because my parents never tried to go back to Hungary to visit, I thought that family wasn't important. Then one day word came that my father's father had died. I saw Dad sitting on the swing alone and crying. I never saw him cry before, but I realized for the first time what a strong tie family is.

Now let us try an easier list.

Dates of Immediate Family

Sept. 6, 1909	Sister, Alice, dies at the age of 11 months
Jan. 11, 1911	Sister, Ethel, born in Brooklyn
May 17, 1914	I was born in the Bronx
Feb. 28, 1919	Wife born in Ross Township, Ohio
July 1, 1944	Wife's father dies at 54
Jan. 30, 1947	Son, Robert, born in Toledo
Aug. 12, 1950	Daughter, Betty, born in Toledo
Aug. 10, 1975	Grandson, Kevin, born in Detroit
Feb. 10, 1978	Father dies at 92
May 19, 1981	Granddaughter, Kori, born in Detroit
Oct. 28, 1982	Mother dies at 93

That list is just filled with memories. It also gives some insight into the kind of person my father was. When he came to Toledo he was instrumental in founding an organization designed to help members in need because of illness and to maintain a cemetery. He remained active in the organization for the rest of his life and both he and my mother are buried in the organization's cemetery. Preparing

for death was very unlike him. Then one day Mom told me a story
that made me understand.

The death of Alice, who was a normal healthy child until
struck down by this ultimately fatal illness, brought great
anger to my father. He could not accept the unfairness.

To make matters worse there seemed to arise some
problem in finding a burial spot in the Jewish cemetery in New
York City. Finding burial space was a common problem. In a
final frustration he threatened to wheel the tiny corpse in her
buggy down to the Battery and right into the Bay. Satisfied
that he meant it, a spot was assigned as a final resting place for
Alice.

Dad wanted to make certain that Mother would never
have to go through such experience again, so he created this
cemetery in Toledo which would be operated free from any
synagogue but in the orthodox tradition.

The list incidentally will be very helpful in determining how
other events fit into the chronological order. Did they happen
before or after so and so's birth and before or after so and so's death?

Residences

About 1915	Family moved from New York to Linwood Avenue in Toledo
About 1919	Kent Street
About 1922	Twelfth Street
About 1923	Lagrange Street
Feb. 11, 1940	Floyd Street
Summer 1941	Franklin Avenue
April 1946	Jackson & Twelfth
June 1948	Back to Lagrange Street
Dec. 18, 1951	Cheltenham Road
May 1984	Ottawa Hills

If you'd like to be more accurate on these dates, you may refer
to old city directories available in libraries and Chamber of

Commerce offices. The directories will not only show where you lived, but they will give you the names of your neighbors, and these may stir the memories a bit.

Under normal circumstances I'd never consider moving into an apartment like the one we took at Jackson and Twelfth Streets. It bordered on downtown, and the neighborhood provided a rich choice of social evils and ailments. I'd just returned from military service, though, and being desperately in need of privacy, the wife and I settled for the first place we could find. As it turned out, we learned to love the place and its people and stayed there until it became evident that our new son needed larger quarters.

Maybe if we'd had any sense we'd have worried about living there, but in a short time we found a friendliness and neighborliness that took us completely by surprise.

You know what it is like when you are ill and your friends and neighbors go out of their way to be helpful and comforting. That's how this neighborhood was except you didn't have to be sick.

The wife became rather close with a neighbor whose husband worked late, would come home drunk, and occasionally beat her. As an alternative she sometimes knocked on our door at 2 a.m. and asked if she could just sit in the living room for a while. He was late coming home, and she knew he'd be drunk. By the time we woke up again she'd be gone.

Early one morning I heard her in our living room talking to my wife. He'd run her out of their apartment with threats. Frankly, I was concerned that he might come up after her, but he never did.

"Why do you stay with him?" the wife demanded. "Why do you put up with him?"

"He's a good man," she replied. "I can't think of myself being without him. I consider staying out of his way when he comes home drunk and angry one of my wifely duties."

I thought my wife would die at that. The neighbor went on.

"See, he's not good with words like your husband is. He

expresses himself best with his hands. He's physical instead of mental, but I've seen women hurt more with words than he's ever hurt me.

"If I'd stayed in the apartment tonight I probably would have gotten a beating, and in the morning he'd be sorry and miserable. I'll go back in a little while and he'll be asleep. In the morning he'll be grateful and relieved that I ran away."

"And how does he express that?" the wife asked flatly.

"With his hands," she replied with a chuckle. "He shows his love with his hands just as positively as he shows his anger."

The wife never could understand that, but I could. I noticed later how quick he was to help with any kind of physical labor, any kind of carrying, and kind of fixing. Anytime he saw a chance to help a neighbor with a chore he was right there, and I concluded that he also showed his neighborliness with his hands.

While I still dislike violence, I think I understand it a lot better now. It is a form of communication, and with some people it is their best form. I'm not saying that you should approve it, but it may be a good idea if you recognize it.

Your school dates also are a productive source of memories and memoirs. Let us list them.

Education

1918–1928	Sherman School
1928–1932	Woodward High School
1932–1936	University of Toledo
June 1937	Northwestern University
1922–1928	Religion Schools

It is during our school years that we leave a long trail of written evidence about our past lives. Grade cards, yearbooks, term papers, and dissertations remind us of what we did, how we thought, by what we were influenced, and how we've changed.

It is also during the school years that we set the course for our lives.

I didn't have an aptitude for language, and resented very much taking Latin. I saw no use for it (although I later found it very useful) and one day I foolishly expressed this opinion in class. The teacher asked me if I could spare five minutes after class.

He was very friendly and even amused as he spoke to me.

"I can give you many reasons why it is useful to study Latin, but let me give you just one. In your case I think it is the most important.

"It is easy to learn something you are eager to learn, but in life you may be faced with having to learn things in which you have no genuine interest. Let Latin be your test of learning something because you must and not because you want to." Then he winked and smiled.

I changed my attitude toward his classes after that, but I don't think it was because of his challenge. I think it was because this was the first time in my life that a teacher approached me as an adult rather than a child, and I think I was returning respect for respect.

In a sense your employment is a continuation of your education. You spent a good part of your life at it, and in a sense it justifies your existence. Of course if you've spent most of your life uneducated and unemployed you may have some very interesting things to say about how you lived.

Employment

1926–1929	Sold newspapers downtown, carried neighborhood routes, sold *Liberty* magazines, sold concessions at ball park, delivered calendars, worked in department store candy kitchen
1929–1936	Worked as high school and university correspondent for morning newspaper, and

	eventually found a job as copyboy on summers and weekends
1936–1937	Sportswriter for afternoon paper
1938–1942	City desk reporter
1943–1946	Military service
1946–1949	City desk again
1949–1969	Sportswriting again
1970–1985	Columnist and feature writer
1960–1975	Founded and operated print shop

I suppose a person learns as much from the people he works for as he does from his school teachers.

I think the first salaried job I ever held was working in the candy kitchen. The candy was sold in bulk. I worked a stand that offered about a dozen different varieties of chocolate-covered goodies.

The rule, explained the straw boss, was that we clerks could eat as much candy as we liked. Being young and gluttonous, I thought this was going to be the greatest job ever invented. Then I discovered after about a half hour of sampling that there was a limit to how much chocolate even a growing boy could eat. There definitely was something like too much of a good thing.

I've often thought back to what a wise policy it was to let the new help eat their fill and get it over with.

The final list of dates deals with special events, and the good times and bad.

Good Times and Bad

1937	A season of unemployment
1937–1939	The courting years
1939–1946	The war years

Sept. 1, 1939	Germany invades Poland
Dec. 7, 1941	Pearl Harbor
Oct. 19, 1943	Drafted into the army
May 16, 1944	Shipped out
May 28, 1944	Landed in Oran, Algeria
June 1944	Assigned to AFHQ in Algiers
June 6, 1944	D-Day in France
July 1944	Shipped to Caserta, Italy
May 4, 1945	V-E Day
Aug. 6, 1945	First atomic bomb dropped
Sept. 6, 1945	V-J Day
Jan. 1946	Shipped back to U.S.
Feb. 6, 1946	Discharged
June 1950	Korean War
Aug. 1964	Vietnam War
1960–1975	Business problems and successes
1975–	Investment successes
1975–1982	Watching parents grow old
March 1975	Parents enter home for aged
Feb. 10, 1978	Father dies
Mar. 14, 1978	Mother blinded by stroke
Oct. 28, 1982	Mother dies

The list of dates you assemble will never be complete, nor will it be completely correct. The first purpose of these dates is to awaken memories.

In a later chapter we will discuss a device for using these dates to get some order to your memoirs.

For the moment, however, the dates are important chiefly as reminders.

Review. Don't expect to develop an event for each date.

Keep adding dates as you run across them or think of them. When you are ready to write your memoirs you may want to list them again in chronological order, but don't think about that now.

VII. Unlocking Your Memories — Facts of Life

The bulk of your autobiography is made up of the facts of your life, the events that influenced it, guided it, and made it what it is today. This chapter will help you gather the facts.

The facts of life represent events that occurred. They may have happened to you, to your family, to your friends, to your ancestors, even to the world in general. The thing you are concerned with is that they affected your life or your outlook on it.

Your memoirs are based from start to finish on these facts. You had foreparents, you were born, you grew up, you lived, you are writing the strongest memories of your life, etc.

You learned much from many of these events, and some of the experiences have been thought-provoking. The lessons and thoughts have been as much a part of your life as the events. You will want to pass them on in your memoirs. They must be stored away in the form of brief notes until you are ready to write them fully.

As you write you will be making a record of the things that happened in it, the lessons they taught you, and any philosophy you may have developed as a result.

At the moment let us concentrate on the facts as compared to the thoughts and lessons — who you are and how you happen to be so.

As you recall an event, you apply the criteria to determine whether the fact is worth saving. Does it advance the story of your life? Is it interesting per se? Does it lead to one of life's lessons? If the answer to any one of these three is yes, make a note of it and stick it in the history envelope for future reference.

If you have any trouble getting started in your collection of facts of life, merely take a look at the dates you've recorded on the separate pages of your tablet. Consider the page headed, "Dates Concerning Forebears."

Where did the family come from? You don't know. Can you guess? Do you have reason to suspect? Didn't your parents ever tell you?

Where did your parents come from? Some sort of statement on forebears is very important, because your ancestors are also your readers, and they'll appreciate any information.

If you don't have facts, maybe you can at least pass on some clues.

The sample list of dates concerning forebears in the previous chapter indicates little information on them. A typical statement in such case might be:

Both of my parents came to the United States from Hungary alone while they were still teenagers. This was not unusual at the time. Getting to America seemed to be the standard solution for a lot of problems. Generally it was assumed either the family would join the child in the new country later or that the child would return when life there was safer for the peasantry. Neither of my parents ever returned or ever saw their parents again.

Dad did talk about getting out of what was then Austria-Hungary on a sort of underground railroad. He and his friends were passed from one "safe" house to another, and crossed the border out of the country where guards were on retainers to look the other way.

In Germany one continued to avoid the authorities, but mostly because it was the nature of life to fear authority, and it was a long and frightening trip to Bremerhaven where the ships to America waited.

This isn't much, but it does account for the family being in the United States, and provides for some sort of a beginning.

Let us pass on to "Dates of Immediate Family."

As a baby Bob was a horrible sleeper. He woke up at all hours of the night, and getting him back to sleep would be an hour's work even for Morpheus. Who would ever dream it was possible to hate someone so much when he was awake and to love him so much when he was asleep.

I'll never forget the first time he slept through the night. I awoke and my room was filled with daylight. My first thought was, "My God, Bobby!! Why isn't he crying?!!"

I leaped out of bed and raced to the nursery. He was soaked, but smiling. I guess he enjoyed the good night's sleep as much as the rest of us.

As I contemplate my grandchildren reading about what a rotten infant their father was, I feel that I have gained my revenge for all those interrupted nights.

Let us now look at a memoir based on events that affected our lives considerably although we had nothing to do with these events directly.

I first learned about the dropping of the atomic bomb on Hiroshima when I was in service in Italy. The Army newspaper, *Stars and Stripes*, reported the event.

I couldn't really absorb the significance of the event beyond the fact that it undoubtedly meant the end of the war and that I'd soon be going home.

When the war ended in Europe a program was set up to release soldiers on a basis of accrued points. Points were given for time in service, battle stars, medals, and the like. I was close to qualifying for release, but not so close that there wasn't a chance of being shipped off to the Pacific where the war was continuing.

The bomb ended that worry for me, but started a lot of other worries for the whole world. The argument whether the United States should have used such a cruel weapon has been

going on since the bomb was dropped, and I had guilt feelings
about benefiting from the bomb that killed so many civilians.

Then many years later I was talking to a man who'd been
a general in the Pacific and who'd been taken to survey the
defenses the Japanese had set up on the mainland in prepara-
tion for the inevitable invasion.

"A lot of Americans and a lot of Japanese would have died
in the invasion. A lot of young people who have been critical
of the bomb wouldn't be here today because their soldier-
fathers would have died on the beaches before they had a
chance to come home and have families," he said.

I think he was absolutely right.

Consider these one by one, and see how many interesting
birthing stories you come up with. One member of our family was
so excited when it came time to take his wife to the hospital that
instead of bringing her suitcase he brought her portable sewing
machine.

Another, a football coach, rushed his wife to the wrong hospital. It was the hospital where his injured football players generally
were taken rather than the one where his wife's doctor waited.

Most of us have sentimental attachment to the houses in which
we lived.

My earliest awareness is of having scarlet fever on Linwood
Avenue. My first experience with death came when a little neighbor
girl died on Kent Street. The neighbors on Twelfth Street owned
a big car, and sometimes I was allowed to sit in it.

Memories of romance and early days of marriage come from
the furnished apartments on the edge of downtown. I remember
each one fondly and distinctly, and they are very helpful in giving
order to my memories.

The general idea is that one can run down the list of dates not
once but many times and never run out of reminders of facts of life
worth telling.

Review. The best way to get started in recalling the events that
shaped your life or, for that matter, knocked it out of shape, is by
studying the list of dates you prepared earlier.

If you really are having trouble finding memoirs, consider each date patiently, think, remember, and you will find something worth writing about.

Talk to others about your memories. Then they will share their memories with you, and that will help you remember even more. It's the way remembering works.

VIII. Unlocking Your Memories — Thoughts of Life

*In writing your memoirs you
will find that recording
your thoughts is far easier
than recording the facts of
your life. How your progeny
see you as a person will be
determined largely by the
thoughts you express.*

This chapter deals with the thoughts of your life as compared to the history and lessons of your life.

Thoughts and lessons sometimes are difficult to separate. One seems to run into another. Don't worry about it. Maybe they shouldn't even be treated separately. The only reason the guide considers them separately is because each provides its own kind of approach to thinking and researching, and two approaches are better than one.

In thinking about lessons, you think of the things that your life's history has taught you, and then necessarily join the two together—what happened and what it taught you.

You don't have to account for your thoughts though. Just think them, and write them. In some cases you may care to point out what inspired them or to justify them with facts based on your experiences. You will cross that bridge when you come to it without even knowing that it is there.

What part do these thoughts play in memoirs?

They permit you to express a philosophy of life.

What else do they do? They give these valued readers of yours a pretty good idea of the kind of person you are.

If you want your readers to think you are nice, give them nice thoughts; if you want them to think you are very nice, give them very nice thoughts; if you want them to think you were a devil, hey, what's wrong with a few devilish thoughts?

I believe that happiness is a legitimate goal in life. Do what will make you happy. The catch is that we don't really know what will make us happy. We may know what will make us happy at the moment, but that really has very little to do with real happiness.

I think I have had more than my share of happiness. Most of it probably has been luck, but some of it has been deliberate.

To begin with, I am naive in most matters. I willingly believe anything I am told — as long as it has no direct effect on my life. Listen. Enjoy. Forget.

I am not talking about listening in a cynical manner, nor a calloused manner, nor a hypocritical manner. Lying is very important to some people. It gives them recognition that they could never get from the truth. If recognition is so important to them that they're willing to lie for it, help them out. Believe their lie. What have you lost?

There is another side to this. Always think twice before telling the truth. In any situation one must always retain the option of lying. The lie in the hands of many people is a formidable weapon. When you make it policy of always telling the truth, you lose the use of this weapon.

This statement makes a rather unusual and certainly controversial point. It supports the lie as a way of life. The problem it creates is that it says to the reader, the writer of these memoirs not only is a liar, but he brags about it. How can we believe this vast amount of information he's left for us? What is truth and what is fiction?

By putting it in your memoirs you've discredited yourself. It is an example of how you will be judged by the thoughts you express.

On the other hand, I enjoy the thought that someday a great-great-grandson of mine might stand up in a public forum and say, "My great-great-granddaddy once said, 'Always think twice before telling the truth,' and I say he is absolutely right." It really doesn't say much, but it sounds awfully wise. Besides it tickles me, and besides that, it is MY memoirs.

Let us consider some more thoughts expressing the philosophy that happiness is the important thing in life.

I have learned to take my beatings when I must with a minimum of fretting. I consider an occasional loss a part of the cost of living. Once a loss is inevitable there is nothing to be gained by dwelling on it. Look around for the next best step and get on with it.

I am basically honest because life is more peaceful that way. All of these things are easier on the nervous system. I sleep better because of them.

I never met a man I was sure I could lick. That keeps me out of more fights than being a law abiding citizen does.

I have a lot of ostrich in me. I try to avoid knowing unpleasant truths unless it is necessary that I know them.

This may not say much for my character, but remember, people who try to avoid unpleasant truths don't start wars, and that ought to be worthy of credit.

These thoughts of yours may take the form of long essays or short throwaway lines, or they may appear at the end of the events that made up your life. For example:

You'd just told a story of a struggle for dominance which you eventually won. You might wrap it up with the statement "The only thing wrong with winning is that it breaks up a lot of interesting fights."

You may want a philosophical outlook toward a rough life. You may write, "Adversity is painful, but it is never boring."

If you've been writing about being neglected by your

children, you can wind up with, "As my mother used to say, if gratitude is so important to you, have puppy dogs instead of sons and daughters."

Let us consider for a moment a seldom-considered aspect of memoirs—the throwaway thought. The word "throwaway" is borrowed from the world of stand-up comedians. The throwaway line is a line a comic can use anytime the spirit moves him. It is short, hopefully clever, and has nothing to do with what he has been saying before or what he will say next.

The throwaway thought is something you've thought of or read someplace that you'd like to pass on, but you have no logical place to put it. Your reason for wanting to pass it on may be because it seems like good advice, or because it makes you sound profound or clever, or because you enjoy it so much you want to share it. If none of these reasons seem to fit, then there is the reason of last resort: These are your memoirs and you can do anything you like with them.

It is strongly suggested, if you have throwaway lines to use, that you scatter them throughout your work. Used here and there they break up the monotony of solid text. Used one after another they contribute to the monotony.

We are all entitled to deeper thoughts, too. We all have them. Why not pass them on?

What do I fear most in death? Not knowing what to fear.

Life balances all things. The greater your wealth, the greater your fear of losing it.

There's a frightening relationship between being free of responsibility and being lonely.

Here are three reasons I am willing to bet that science will find a way to control atomic energy. First, if I lose who will be here to collect? Second, if I lose, who will be here to pay, and third, if I lose what will there be to pay with?

If someone gave me a choice of either keeping my telephone or my television set, I'd knock him down.

People without children feel sorry for people with children. People with children feel sorry for people without children. It's a perfect arrangement.

If you are given the choice of luck or skill in raising your children, take luck. It's the only chance in the world of raising them right.

A man should retire as early as he can or as late as he can. Anything in between is uncertainty.

I believe in Santa Claus. He is a force that makes parents want to do nice things for children who have been good.

It is my firm belief that the descendants of the people who are horrified by the development of atomic energy were horrified by the development of natural gas heating, gasoline engines, kerosene lamps, wind-powered sailing ships, the wheel, and fire.

Finding a peaceful use for the atom is a big order considering that man hasn't even found a peaceful use for the bullet yet.

My generation's contribution to the world was the atomic bomb. Your generation's contribution may well be ashes.

We all have our needs. Some people have a need to be greedy.

Be fair. Should a man be deprived of the pleasures of wanting just because he has everything?

One of my four uncles was very selfish, very greedy, and very rich, but somehow he got a lot more attention from us than any of the other three.

Aging is better than nothing.

My mother said she was 85 before she really felt old, and by then she didn't want to do anything young people do anyhow.

While the thoughts that come from inspiration as you write are probably the best thoughts, there is a way of deliberately conjuring up thoughts. It is best practiced in small groups. One then becomes proficient in doing it by himself.

At the end of this book is a word game. It is included because it is a fine device for stimulating the conversation and thinking. Pick any word as a subject. The idea then is for one person to voice an opinion on that subject, and someone else to tell him why he is wrong.

Generally the original word will soon be forgotten but the ideas, thoughts, and memories generated by the conversation it started will provide grist for the memoir mill.

Review. Your thoughts, your opinions will tell your readers more about who you were and what you were like than your history ever will.

Use your thoughts to create the image you'd like them to have of you.

Your thoughts may be long essays, short paragraphs, or merely throwaway lines that give your readers something to think about.

If you're stuck, take a look at the word list in the back of this book. In group writing, when all else fails to inspire thought, that list will succeed.

IX. Unlocking Your Memories — Lessons of Life

> *Your memoirs should teach the reader something. At least we should give him an opportunity to learn from the lessons our lives taught us.*

In this chapter we hope to learn how to discern the lessons our lives have taught us, and to pass them on in our memoirs.

While we learn a great deal from experience, in most cases we take the lessons for granted, and unless we think very hard about it we have trouble recognizing that a lesson had been learned.

Let us start with an example. The two incidents recorded here happened 62 years apart. Yet, I know for a fact that they were related.

When I was a little boy my father smoked a cigarette-shaped cigar called "Between the Acts." They came in shallow tin boxes, and as Dad emptied each box he would give it to me to play with.

The truth of the matter is that is wasn't much as playthings go. The box smelled strongly from tobacco. The odor transferred to my hands and was unpleasant. The edges were sharp, and there really wasn't much a little boy could do with so shallow a box. Yet, he always passed them down to me, and I always accepted them.

One evening he casually handed an empty box to my

sister instead. I was very hurt. I suppose I'd grown to feel Dad's giving me the empty boxes as a recognition of my place in the family, and when he gave it to my sister instead — she was several years older and certainly had even less use for the smelly things than I did — it was as if I'd been replaced in his heart. I don't recall that I said or did anything about it, but I was very hurt.

Some years later I was visiting my four-year-old grandson, and found him entertaining three friends. I had several novelty pencils with me, and was about to give one to each child when I remembered the cigar box. I passed four of the pencils on to my grandson, and suggested that he give one to each of his friends and keep one for himself. Proudly he did so.

The lesson here is that you belong to your children (or grandchildren) at least as much as they belong to you. Whether they wish to share you with their friends is a decision for them to make. If I'd given the pencils to my grandson's little friends directly, it would say to his four-year-old mind that I loved them as much as I loved him.

Is this lesson worth passing on to the progeny? I certainly hope so. I've been passing it on to anyone who would listen for years.

I learned not to smoke from a single experience that had nothing to do with the evils of smoking.

My earliest days in the newspaper business came when most cities still had newspapers in competition with each other and speed was as important if not more important than accuracy.

I was a copyboy, but the city editor sent me out with a regular reporter to cover a very violent strike. Two men had been killed, and the National Guard was firing tear gas all over the place. We were to go out, grab what information we could get, and hurry back to make the early edition.

We got back with the odor of tear gas still in our clothing, our nostrils, and our eyes. The reporter sat down at the typewriter. I stood by him with my notes. I was excited about being sent out, and wanted to do the job.

The reporter adjusted his hat, rolled paper into the typewriter, and was about to begin when he decided he needed a cigarette. He searched through three pockets and finally found the pack. He flipped a cigarette into his mouth, and poised to type again. Then he decided he needed a match. That took some time.

He lit up and finally began typing, but the smoke from the cigarette began irritating his already irritated eyes. He carefully put the cigarette down on the edge of the desk and reached for his handkerchief. Then the cigarette rolled away, and he had to grab at it to stop it.

By this time the city editor was asking for the story. Now the reporter started pounding away, came up with three quick pages, and then turned them in without even asking me about the notes I'd picked up.

I was disappointed, angry, and frustrated. I could do nothing to get even with the veteran reporter, so I did the next best thing. I got even with the tobacco companies. I never smoked.

Most of my lessons came from the newspaper business. I learned how to deal with committees from meetings I covered.

Youngsters had rioted at a lake resort one Fourth of July, and the police chief ordered the main street blocked, the amusement park darkened, and the shops closed until order could be restored.

County deputies came in to help, some arrests were made, and that ended the holiday weekend. From the business standpoint, this was supposed to be the two days that the businesses turned their profits, but there was to be no such thing.

I covered the meeting of merchants that followed, and listened as many of them bitterly castigated the chief and threatened to organize an impeachment movement against the mayor.

The raging lasted for 45 minutes without one logical, unemotional argument being presented, but now was dying under the weight of repetition of charges and sagging energy.

Then the doughnut shop man stood up. "Gentlemen," he said, "I believe that the main business of this meeting is to see that we do not have another repetition of the violence that caused this unfortunate situation.

"I suggest that we ask the chief to set up a program to train volunteers to work with him much as the fire department has volunteers. With such help potential troublemakers can be spotted and brought under control before their mischief spreads. I will be the first to volunteer."

The rest of the audience, relieved to hear a bit of common sense, and eager to get home, applauded, and the meeting broke up leaving everyone with a sense of accomplishment.

I used this experience in serving on committees later. If there was something I really wanted accomplished in the face of considerable opposition. I would wait until everybody was talked out, and then lay out my plan calmly, voicing no opposition to what had been said, but talking as if I were the first speaker of the evening.

Sometimes it worked.

One way to understand lessons as a part of life is to start out with the question, "What is the most important lesson you've learned in life?" Follow this question with the question, "Why do you say that?" Then you're on your way.

Review. We've learned a lot of lessons in our lives, but unless we give it a lot of thought we don't realize that we've learned them from experience. We feel like we just naturally know it.

Try the two questions suggested in the last paragraph of this chapter to give yourself an awareness of what life has taught you.

X. Recording the Great Event

*Many of us have been marked
for good or evil by one life-
changing experience, a single
factor so great and so important
that it overshadows all
else. In this chapter we examine
how to deal with the
great events in our lives.*

While your memoirs may be made up of rather commonplace events, in many lives there is at least one great event which had special significance and which requires a different treatment from the other memoirs.

It is some one thing that changed the course of your life. It may well be your reason for wanting to preserve your memoirs.

Some examples:

• You started a small business and built it into a major commercial venture, establishing a family fortune, and bringing about considerable change in the family's life style for at least a generation to come.

• You committed a major crime, were caught, and wasted a lot of good years in jail.

• You were handicapped by an accident, and had to learn how to live an entirely different kind of life than you had planned.

• You worked your way up to the head of an important company.

• You were a star in the field of athletics or entertainment.

- You served in a high elective office.
- Your marriage, your divorce, your second marriage or whatever changed your life.
- You gained national fame through a book, an act of heroism, whatever.

Because of its importance, this deserves treatment more elaborate than the bulk of your memoirs. It may test your skill as a writer a bit more than the rest of your work, but you will find the instructions that follow will lead you to an easy way to handle the task at hand.

The heart of these instructions is that you collect the dates, actual or approximate, and match the events with them. Then you tell the story in chronological order after introducing it with a brief statement.

An example may prove helpful. Let us start with dates.

June 1, 1936. Graduate with a degree in mechanical engineering.

July 14, 1936. Find work as a draftsman, but it is temporary.

Sept. 1936. Take another temporary job. Very depressing. Some fellow graduates selling shoes.

Dec. 1938. Feel strongly that life is passing me by. Have lost touch with engineering. Think about opening a grocery store. Parents offer some financial help.

Feb. 1939. Find a small store in factory district. Remain open the unheard of hours of 6:30 a.m. to midnight in order to catch all three shifts of factory workers.

Jan. 1940. Store is free of debt. Find time to get married.

Feb. 1941. We're at war. Entry into service is inevitable. Wife and parents pitch in at store.

July 1941. Drafted into army. Store doing rather well.

Nov. 1945. Return from service full of new ideas for store.

Feb. 1946. Notified by landlord I will have to move. Bank wants to buy store for own use. Nothing available in neighborhood. It's a real blow.

May 1946. I'm out. Fixtures in storage.

Aug. 1946. Find large store on edge of town. It means

rebuilding whole new business. Hate to think of it, but a family is on the way. Got to do something.

Oct. 1946. New store opened. No factory traffic here. Experience marketing problem. Radio advertising not enough.

Jan. 1947. Experimenting with direct mail. Results seem to be good, but it takes a lot of running between printer and post office.

Feb. 1948. Too tired to take copy to printer. Decide to try daily paper instead. First ad draws very well but is expensive.

March 1948. Suggest to independent grocer across town that we advertise together, split cost. Find three other widely separated grocers to join in.

April 10, 1948. First full-page ad. Everybody does big business. Coordinating difficult.

May 1948. Hire part-time advertising man. Set up ground rules for meetings. Reach agreement on making contributions for administrative services.

May 1949. Hire fulltime advertising and marketing director. Big business now. Building a second store.

May 1950. Running into serious problems. Some advertising partners don't want to grow. Satisfied with ma-and-pa operation. Can't compete with chains unless they build larger stores.

June 1951. Everybody making more money than they ever dreamed, but being held back by the smaller stores. Wondering about throwing our stores together into one chain, and taking stock in return.

May 1952. Finally get down to serious business of becoming a genuine chain operation. Selling the idea that it will mean more time to enjoy the money we are making. Hire outside firm to study how much each store is worth and come up with plan for exchanging stock for store.

Dec. 1952. First proposal completed. Can see larger store-owners will have to sweeten it to sell it to the smaller ones.

April 1953. Spending lot of time talking to each owner individually. Talk more about what he wants to do with the rest of his life than how much he wants for store. All thinking more sensibly now. Even me.

Summer 1953. We're meeting socially more—that means the wives, too. The climate for considering incorporation into a single firm is much better. The idea for having more time for boating and golf is catching on.

Jan. 1954. Deal finally completed. We're all executives of Consumer Foods instead of store-owners. First business is opening more stores. Looking for managerial help from among the old employees. The sooner we get old employees into old stores the better.

Jan. 1956. Annual report looks great. Have fended off every effort of chains to hurt us. Don't even feel like we're on the defensive anymore.

Jan. 1960. Tired. We're too big. Everything is numbers. The inspiration is gone. I'd like to sell out and retire, but my only customer would be the corporation, and it doesn't have enough money.

July 1960. After studying how a firm goes public I have offered a suggestion that Consumer offer its stock on the open market. Having all our wealth in one business is really risky. If we go public we can sell some of our stock and hold on to some. I said I will put all my stock up and get out of the business.

Oct. 1961. The deal is finally completed. We have gone public. I should have my money in two months. I can't believe it. My accountant says it will be $2 million after taxes. I'm scared to death. It's a whole new world. I hope I like it.

This is the outline. Most dates are approximate. Needless to say, the events loom large in the writer's mind. There is little need for research except possibly to look up a few dates.

Now let us convert this to language suitable for insertion in the autobiography. We start with introductory comment.

I never meant to be wealthy. I mean it wasn't in my plans. I assumed that I would make a comfortable living, but that's as far as serious thinking ever took me.

I entered the university and took engineering. I don't know exactly why. It just looked better than anything else. Actually, we were deep in the Depression at the time, and nothing one could study would guarantee a future or even a job.

I finished rather high in the class, was interviewed by

several local firms, but the best any one of them could offer was a draftsman's board. Maybe something better would turn up later. It didn't. The company was out of work after three months, and so was I.

A week later I was called in by another firm for a job scheduled to last a month. It lasted two. Actually, I was lucky. Many of my classmates were selling shoes. Between engineering jobs I found I could get selling jobs in the wholesale food industry. My parents had a grocery store, and I grew up with the business.

Selling, however, turned out to be a lot of driving, a lot of walking, a lot of lifting, and a lot of disappointment.

I couldn't help notice that despite a scarcity of jobs in the field, the university continued to turn out engineers. It meant that the competition for jobs was getting tougher, and I was getting nowhere. I'd been out of school for two years with nothing to show for it. Life was passing me by.

It didn't help that I'd met the girl I wanted to marry, and as an unemployed engineer I was having trouble impressing her folks.

By Christmas of 1938 I started talking about going into some kind of business for myself—maybe a grocery store. I don't know if I really meant what I was saying. I certainly didn't think much of the life my father lived, getting up early in the morning to go to market, sleeping a few hours in the afternoon, and working until eight p.m. at the store.

Yet, I couldn't remain unemployed. My parents offered to help me financially. The least I could do is look.

In February of 1939 I found a building on the busy intersection of a factory district. The rent was right. I could lease it month to month. If things got too bad I could pull out.

In three weeks I had the place ready for business. By staying open from 6:30 a.m. to midnight I could catch all three shifts going and coming from the factories. It didn't take long to catch on. I was busy most of the time, and tired all the time. Yet I felt very good about myself.

In less than a year the store was free of debt, and I had the money and found the time to get married.

Then came Pearl Harbor and the war. It was inevitable that I'd be drafted soon. I started teaching my new wife the business so that she could take care of it while I was gone. My parents pitched in, too.

I went into the Army in July of 1941 and came out in November of 1945 full of new ideas for the store. I had some ideas about knocking out a wall for expansion and building a parking lot nearby. The supermarket was a coming thing.

It wasn't to be, however. In February, 1946, I was told that I would have to move. The bank that previously had occupied the building was coming back in. They needed this particular building because the walls were reinforced, and all they would have to do was put the vault door back on the room I'd been using as an office. Actually it was a safe.

There was absolutely nowhere else in the neighborhood that I could move. The business I'd built up had nowhere to go but down the drain. I put my fixtures in storage, and wondered whether I'd been away from engineering too long to return.

But then I found a large vacant store on the edge of town which seemed to have some promise. It had a parking lot attached, and would make a slightly smaller version of a supermarket. I borrowed money from the bank, and opened. That was in October.

There was no factory traffic out that way, so I'd have to find some new marketing techniques. I'd used radio advertising at the old store, but that didn't do much in the new location. I turned to direct mail.

The direct mail did the job, but it involved a great deal of planning and running and addressing and mailing, and the wife and I did most of it.

One week I'd neglected to get the copy to the local printer in time. I knew that I couldn't face a weekend without advertising of some kind, so I called the newspaper, although I felt that advertising for a single store in a paper of such broad circulation was a waste of money.

As it turned out the newspaper drew very well.

If I could find another grocer in a far part of town who

wanted to advertise with me I could cut costs and increase the size of the ad.

I found one in the far West End, and after several meetings we agreed that there seemed to be a future in joint advertising but we needed more stores. We soon found three other grocers, and were running full page ads.

Needless to say, handling advertising for five stores with five different owners had its complications. Each store had had to be certain to have plenty of whatever was to be advertised, and we sometimes ran short. This, of course, was bad for the image of the group. Furthermore, several stores didn't know how to handle the traffic the ads were drawing to move the more profitable items along with the advertising leaders.

It soon was obvious that to do the job right we would need a fulltime advertising and marketing director. We were big now, but we also had large overheads, larger than some of the storeowners were used to handling.

In May of 1950 I became aware of a serious problem. Rather blindly I'd assumed that everybody in the advertising arrangement wanted to grow bigger, but that was not the case. We had some ma-and-pa stores who were perfectly happy with their operations, and wanted no part of the obligations that come with growing. Yet, we had to grow. We'd reached the point where we were challenging the chain stores, and they were getting ready to move into our areas and swallow us. They could do it if our stores stayed small.

I got nowhere with my arguments. All of us actually were making more money than they'd ever had before, and most were satisfied. They couldn't understand that either we continued to grow or we'd die. There was no such thing as standing still.

It was evident that the only way we could survive was to incorporate as a single business made up of all the stores. Each owner would have to turn his store over to the corporation in exchange for stock. This would free the corporation to enlarge stores, add stores, or do whatever was necessary to maintain its share of the market.

It took a lot of doing, but I finally got permission to hire a firm to study how much each store was worth, and come up with a plan for exchanging stores for stock. That was in May of 1952.

When a preliminary study was issued the following December it was evident that we larger storeowners would have to sweeten the pot for the smaller ones.

To this point I'd been doing a lot of haranguing about the necessity to consolidate. I was making everyone uncomfortable and a lot of people resentful. Now I changed my approach. I don't know if I did it as a matter of strategy or because I didn't like being disliked. There were good, honest, and hardworking people. They seemed to think I was trying to take their stores away from them — and I guess I was, even though it was for their own good.

I spent more time getting to know the owners as individuals rather than businessmen. We'd talk about what we wanted for our stores. That led to a lot more sensible thinking from all of us, including me.

We started getting together socially — the wives, too. The climate for considering more free time through consolidation improved. The idea of having more time for boating and golf and travel made more sense under those conditions.

In January of 1954 we finally reached an agreement on consolidation. It meant that Consumer Foods would be a true corporation instead of merely an advertising and marketing co-op. Every former owner became an executive officer in the corporation, but it was hard to stop thinking of the old store as "my" store, and it took a great deal of tact and diplomacy to keep everyone happy.

We built new stores, and enlarged the old ones, and by promoting all the partners' favorite employees to better jobs in the new stores, the confidence and morale of those who worried about the consolidation were elevated considerably.

By January of 1956 we were in great shape. Our annual report was beautiful. We'd fended off all efforts of the chains to hurt us, and did a little hurting ourselves. We'd crossed the city lines, the county lines, and the state lines.

I think that's when I started losing interest in the business.

We'd grown too large. I couldn't seem to keep my thumb on anything. I spent most of my time looking at someone else's numbers. Even if I understood what they said, I'm not sure I would know where to go to do something about them. I began to think about retiring.

It was not in my nature to leave my large investment in a business that someone else was going to run. The only way I would get out would be to cash my stock in, and the corporation didn't have enough money to handle such a deal. I started reading on how to go public. At the July, 1960, board meeting I offered a suggestion that we consider offering Consumer Food stock on the open market.

Inasmuch as we've done so well, I argued, we now find ourselves with practically all our money in a single business. This is unnecessarily risky.

I agreed that I would put up all my stock for sale as a method of entering the market, and that if the others wanted to sell their stock now or later they'd have a market where it could be done. The plan was studied, and eventually accepted pretty much as I had presented it.

On October 4, 1961, a deal was completed with a bond house to put the stock on the market, and I was informed that I would have my money within 60 days. My accountant informed me that it would be over $2 million after taxes.

I did a strange thing after I got the news. I went out, sat in the car, and cried. I haven't the slightest idea why, but if you ever wonder what the reaction of a man is when he's money-rich that's one of them.

Two months later I was up to my ears in happy work, making investments, setting up trusts, and discovering how happily busy having money can keep one.

This is a long and detailed description of the founding of a family fortune. Yet it is a simple and factual report of what happened. Undoubtedly elsewhere in the memoirs will appear lessons and thoughts generated by this project.

Review. One or two events may stand out in your life above all others. They will deserve more elaborate treatment. They will be a bit more complicated to handle.

The easy method is to reduce the events to a series of dates as outlines, and then tell each simply and directly from beginning to end.

XI. Deciding Who You Are and What You Are Trying to Say

*The time has come to think.
It will be helpful to know
who you are and what you
are trying to say to these
unknown kinfolk of yours.
Once you reach these decisions,
the rest is easy.*

You've probably had fun collecting facts, talking about yourself and your life, putting your thoughts down on paper, and working toward completing a mission. You now have several envelopes fat with notes, and some very good ideas about who you are and what you would like to say to these future generations of yours.

Now there are a few things to think about, some decisions to make before you start your final draft.

The first of these is: *How do you wish to appear to these future generations of yours?* How would you like your readers to think of you, to picture you?

What they will think of you depends entirely on what you say and how you say it.

Let us consider a possibility.

I'm the Foxy Grandpa type. All things considered I did pretty well. I didn't make much money, but I had a lot of fun. Most of my wisdom came from the streets. I am pretty intelligent, and if circumstances had permitted me to go to college I probably would have been a doctor or a lawyer or an engineer, and I'd probably have been a good one.

But I have no regrets. There is a great deal to be said for living by one's wits, and knowing that you're going to eat well and sleep warm no matter where you are. You can take care of yourself.

Would I advise my readers to follow my course? Of course not. They'd never make it on the streets. They're not me.

Now let us look at the kind of a memoir a Foxy Grandpa might include to show the kind of character he is:

When I was about 13 I was caught stealing cough medicine from a neighborhood drug store. To this day I can't tell you why I took it, except that it was out in the open, and when I picked the bottle up it felt good in my hand. I stuck it in my belt at the small of my back where it was covered by my jacket.

I didn't see the pharmacist who was behind a tall counter, but he saw me, and soon he had me in hand. I started crying because it seemed to be a good idea. Then the manager asked me a question that gave me an opener.

"Why in the world are you stealing cough syrup?" he asked. "There are at least a hundred things in this store that a kid your age would prefer to cough syrup."

It was a good question. I thought of a good answer.

"It's for my little brother," I said. "He coughed all night last night. We don't have money, so I stole it."

He seemed to buy the story. The manager took the bottle away and loosened his grip on my neck.

"I could use a kid like you around here," he said. "It's too bad you can't be trusted."

"If I had a job and had money to buy what I needed, you would never have to worry about me stealing," I replied, "and I'd work hard."

He handed the bottle back to me, and said, "Come in after school tomorrow. I'll let you earn that cough medicine. Take it home. Your brother needs it."

I went back the next day, and had my first day's work. I enjoyed it. I liked looking at all the different things they sold there. When my friends came in and saw me working, it made me important.

I continued going in after school, and he always found work for me. I was getting 25 cents an hour, and everything was just great. I was even thinking of becoming a pharmacist when I grew up.

One day a couple of weeks later my mother came into the store, and while she was talking to me the manager came up and told her what a good worker I was.

Then he asked how my little brother was doing. This surprised Mom considerably. See, I don't have a little brother, just an older sister.

Well to make a long story painful, when she left the manager turned on me. "Get out," he said. "You're not only a thief, but you're a liar too."

I was heartbroken. Of course, I lied, but that was only to get out of the trouble I was in. Hadn't I proved anything since?

I really think that's what embittered me, and led me to the kind of life I eventually had. I suppose I should be grateful. If I'd been a pharmacist, I probably wouldn't have any memoirs worth preserving.

Can you see what this memoir did? It provided a reason for your being a street man instead of a solid citizen. It showed that you really could have made it, except for some straight guy not recognizing a good employee when he had one.

Let's build another character for you.

I am a very ordinary person in my own eyes. I seemed to have raced through life with nothing spectacular to show for it, although maybe there's something spectacular about being a good wife and mother.

I think there are millions of people very much like me, and when I speak for myself I speak for them. I worked for what I got, and I never got something for nothing. On the other hand I never needed something for nothing.

My husband and I lived within our means and raised our children to do the same. My memoirs should provide a good idea of how the average solid family lived in the 20th century.

Sometimes I am ashamed that I didn't travel more, didn't learn more, and didn't accomplish more in my lifetime, yet I don't see how anyone could have had a more busy life than I did, caring for a husband and raising and educating three children.

When my friends talk of their travels to Europe and China, I'd like to explain to them that I never felt the need to get away like that. I had everything I needed right where I was. Tell the truth, what are the reasons for going off to the far corners of the world? Are you bored? Do you have nothing useful to offer at home? Maybe it is to your credit to get out and meet new and different people, but there are plenty of those right around the corner.

Now let us look at some of the memoirs that might suggest themselves to this stay-at-home type. A safe memoir always is how I met my husband and how he happened to propose to me.

I was 24 and working as a salesgirl in dresses at the Rhinebolt department store when my husband, Bill, proposed to me. We'd gone together steadily for two years, and there was no one else in our lives. It's amazing how used to a person you can get in two years.

I was still living at home, but I was spending more time in his car than I was in the house. That's how it was in those days. Not many young people could afford apartments. The closest thing to privacy we could get would be in cars.

I'd just gotten in my mind the fact that I'd like to be a buyer. For a long time I felt I knew more about what the customers in our store liked than our buyer did. I could pick out what dresses would go first when the new garments came in, and I seldom was wrong. Some of the stuff that came in I didn't even want to see on the racks. I knew that if I were given a chance as a buyer I'd do very well.

Buyers always wore smart clothes, extreme hairdos, and

went a little heavy on makeup. Maybe it made them feel more important than the salesgirls when they came around to tell us what lines to display. I started wearing more makeup, and going into the store salon for styling, and I even picked up some dresses that were a little extreme for me. I decided that this was my best chance of being noticed in case a buyer job opened up. Buyers were transferred around the chain quite often.

Well, the first to notice me was Bill. He picked me up at work. It was the first time he saw me all made up and everything. That night he proposed. I asked him to give me time to think. He said okay. That night he was ready to give me anything.

As I took the makeup off I became furious. All these months I'd been his clean, neat girlfriend, and nothing happened. One time he sees me all floozied up, and he's ready to marry me! What kind of husband is that? He's marrying me for my makeup.

I went to bed telling myself all the things I was going to say to him the next time we dated, and I wasn't at all certain there was going to be a next time. Of the things I was going to say to him one of them was not going to be "yes."

The next day I was putting on my makeup when I was struck by a whole new thought about Bill. There really was no question in my mind that we loved each other, and if with a little makeup and a bit of hairspray I can get him eating out of my hand, what's wrong with that?

We set a date, and got married. I quit work to become a housekeeper, and until the kids started coming, I would always meet him at the door with my hair combed and just a little more makeup on than I should be wearing.

It's funny how much pleasure you can get from pleasing the one you love.

Say you are a thoughtful, tolerant and responsible member of society whose life has been made more interesting by your efforts to understand religious and cultural differences which set us so much apart from each other.

You want to deliver the message: Make your life more

interesting by recognizing the differences and studying them. The alternative, fighting them, just leads to frustration and unhappiness.

A memoir like the one that follows would establish such characteristics in you.

> I have spent a great deal of time pondering religion. This is a very interesting thing to do because it is completely subjective. I don't have to know anything about religion. All I have to do is to know how I feel about it.
>
> My conclusions are many and confused. I find myself believing in God when it gives me comfort to do so. My sense of logic tells me there is no God. Yet, why do I spell His name with a capital G?
>
> There are so many mysteries, so many things that defy explanation — the working of man's mind, the endlessness of the universe, the infinite varieties of living creatures — that it is easier to believe in God than to figure it all out.
>
> I definitely value the civilizing effect of religion. If a group of infants were placed on an island and managed to survive with no outside influence, I firmly believe that they quickly would establish a religion. It probably would be based on the sun. The sun's effect on us is so obvious. When it is present we have warmth, light and growth. In its absence we have cold, darkness and fear.
>
> Great crimes have been committed in the name of religion as ambitious men sought more power for themselves.

Once you have determined how you would like to appear in the eyes of this future generation of yours, you try to make certain that you write nothing that would be out of character for one of that image.

How important is this?

In real life we are complex characters, and while in most ways we remain rather consistent, occasionally we do something out of character. A man of the cloth tells a dirty joke. A man of integrity peeks at his neighbor's cards. A loving husband finds himself thinking of loving someone else.

These inconsistencies don't work well in books. They are too hard to follow, and the character becomes unbelievable. In books villains must be villains and heroes, heroes, and if a hero participates in a bit of villainy he must have a good reason for it or it will confuse his readers.

So it is in these memoirs you plan to leave behind. Decide the kind of character you want to be and if you find the need to shift gears, make certain you provide a good reason for doing so or show proper regret for having done so.

A second decision is, *What message do I have for this future generation of mine?*

Is a message necessary? Probably not, but most fine pieces of writing have messages tucked away in them. These needn't be important, nor do they have to be obvious. The message gives the memoir a reason for being.

To a creative soul, the cruellest retort in the world is the two-word question, "So what?" The message in your works provides the answer to that cruel question. It goes even further. It makes it unnecessary that the question be asked.

If you feel a need to test each memoir, when you finish it ask yourself, "So what?" If the answer is "So laugh" or "So learn" or "So enjoy" it's a good memoir, and it has a message.

Let us consider some examples of messages:

Life is a battle. Come out fighting, and be ready to protect yourself at all times.

Set goals and keep your eyes on them.

Life is shorter than you think.

There is much pleasure to be gained from spreading joy.

In facing any issue, always think first about how important it is, and then react accordingly. Don't waste time, energy and material or make a point just as a matter of principle. Don't let anybody but God give you a heart attack.

The last one is my favorite. It was one of the many things I learned from Dad. I'd gotten into a fight at school and came home with my shirt torn. As a rule I didn't win many fights, but this time the other kid ran home crying.

"So you won the fight," Dad said. "Toby ran home crying."

"He certainly did," I assured him.

"Well," he said. "I'm sure he's not crying anymore — but your shirt is still torn."

Suddenly I realized what a waste the whole thing was. In my adult years I've asked myself many times, what are the possible rewards of this effort and are they worth it. Sometimes I even let myself be guided by the answer.

Now let us consider the third and final decision. *Try to create in your mind an image of the people for whom you are writing.*

It is much easier to write, if you pretend you know the people who will be reading your work.

In my case I think of a young married couple. At first I tried to take into consideration the fact that this will be a hundred years from now and everything will be different. That became too hard to handle. By then our television may have been replaced by some sort of exist-o-vision where you are actually a part of what is tranpiring on television. I just take the attitude that life is still pretty much like it is today, and let it go at that.

I suppose that who you are writing for depends on how old you are and many other factors. If I were doing my memoirs from prison I'd probably pretend I am writing to youngsters who can use all the advice I can give them about the straight and narrow.

If I were an invalid I think I would be writing to youngsters to whom I would be trying to convey some insight into and feeling for shut-ins.

Pick your own victims, and think you are writing directly to them as you write.

Review. It will be very helpful if you can determine: (1) the image of yourself you'd like to convey, (2) the message you wish to send, and (3) the people for whom you are writing. Use the "So what" test in evaluating each memoir.

XII. Fitting It All Together

This chapter deals with organizing your notes, and figuring out what goes where. It can be exciting or it can be tedious depending upon how eager you are to see your memoirs take form.

The following is very important. Please read it carefully.

There are two ways to go from here in the completion of your memoirs.

If you would like your memoirs to take the form of your life story, you follow one route. If you would like your memoirs to be a series of unrelated albeit interesting notes, you follow another.

Life will be simpler if you elect to go the unrelated note route, but there may be more satisfaction in telling a complete story of your life.

Take either route for a start. You can always change your mind.

Let us first talk about presenting your memoirs in an autobiographical manner, as a complete life story. If you are good at jigsaw puzzles that should be a breeze.

What we are dealing with here is creating an outline in your manuscript. Get the envelope marked *Dates* and make a list of the dates in chronological order. Some compromising may be necessary, but perfection is not a requirement. If your list is roughly accurate, that is all that is necessary.

You will find a sample outline at the end of this chapter that may be some help to you.

Now turn your attention to the contents of your *History*
envelope. Spread your notes out before you. Next examine the
notes in your *Lessons* envelope. Look at them one by one and see
if they are related to your *History* notes. If so clip them together
and write them as one.

Do the same with the notes in your *Thoughts* and *Miscellany*
envelopes. Where ideas seem to mesh, clip the notes together.

At this point you have piles of notes related to raising children,
business ventures, religion, growing up, love, marriage, and on and
on. The idea is that you now have your life before you in logical
piles. Each pile probably will contain information on the events that
happened, the lessons they taught you, and your observations about
the whole thing.

Now turn your attention back to the chronological list you've
organized. Fit each pile of notes that lends itself to being dated in
the order suggested by your chronological outline.

Now take the notes that don't — and these will be mostly from
your *Thoughts* and *Miscellany* envelopes and insert them where
logic tells you they will fit. What you have left over you may include
in a catchall section at the end of your biography under a title like
"Random Notes," or "Thoughts Left Over from a Long, Hard
Life."

When you are satisfied with your distribution of your notes,
put them somewhere that they will be safe. I suggest putting each
pile between the individual pages of your self-adhesive album as a
safe storage place until you are finished with them. That way neither
the notes nor their order is likely to be disturbed.

At last you are ready to start writing for your manuscript. We
bring it up now because it is something you do not have in your
notes. It is some very necessary information to be used as a preface
in order to answer four questions of extreme importance to your
readers.

They are: Who am I? When am I writing this? Why am I
writing this? What is my situation at the time I am writing this?

The answer to the first need be little more than your name,
although you may want to deal with family affiliations so that the
reader will know from the start how you fit into his or her family.
A typical example:

My name is Mrs. Helen Hubert. I was born Helen Jensen in 1907. My husband was John Hubert. His family helped settle the Newmark, Indiana, area. The Huberts are still numerous in that part of the state.

The answer to the second question need only be a date at the head of the manuscript—or at the end. Yet, even this may be elaborated.

I am writing this in the year 1984, a year that probably will go down in history only for the uncertainty of this country's foreign relations.

While we are at peace we seem to be involved in some secret wars in the Middle East and in Central America.

It really is a transition year in which we seem to be going somewhere, but nothing conclusive has happened.

The answer to the third question will vary greatly. The answer lies in part in the statement you wrote for yourself in the previous chapter, the statement in which you decided for yourself what message you hoped to convey.

A few examples:

I am writing this mostly because I would like to start a record of the Jensen-Hubert family. Possibly later Huberts and Jensens who read this will update it with the story of their own lives, and thus keep the family history going for generations. I think it helps one find a direction for his life if he knows the kind of people he comes from.

In my lifetime I have developed a philosophy which made living a joy. I learned to roll with the punches, I learned to correct the unpleasantnesses when I could, and to ignore them if I couldn't. I made it a practice not to waste precious time and energy fighting something I couldn't beat. The secret was in the ability to wipe from my mind anything I didn't want there. I honestly believe that this played an important part in keeping me healthy, happy and alive.

By most standards I have been successful. I have done well in business, I have participated in civic work, and I raised and educated a family at some sacrifice, a fact that even some of the people close to me seemed to overlook.

I like to think that my life marked the beginning of a dynasty for the family and that it was the start of finer things to come. I like to think that someday the accomplishments of one of my descendants will justify a biography or biographies, and that these memoirs will provide source material for his beginnings.

I contracted polio at the age of three and do not remember the time I wasn't handicapped. I am aware that the older I got the more difficult life became. As a child I got a lot of attention from my parents and my brothers and sisters. As they died, or left, I became less and less a part of their lives. I managed to achieve a college degree which was a great source of satisfaction to me, but I am not certain that having accomplished this it didn't add to my frustrations because I was given so little opportunity to make full use of what I knew.

I suppose I am writing this largely as something to do, yet I hope without hope that it will provide some worthwhile insight of what it is truly like to be handicapped.

Let us see how these four might answer the fourth question, What is my situation at the time I am writing this?

Mrs. Hubert might write,

I am 76 now and living comfortably in my own apartment in a complex designed for the elderly. The children call me frequently and seem to have genuine concern for my welfare. I seem to be much luckier than many people my age because in addition to having my children, I also have my health. I can't believe that I really am old, but to be honest, I realize that I could no longer compete in society. It is in this rather pleasant state of mind and body that I am beginning to write my memoirs.

As for the second writer, the one who has a philosophy to expound, he may answer the fourth question as follows:

> I am 64, a bit heavy, and somewhat happy with my life. I still look at women and think about girls a lot. I am in selling, and plan to retire in a year or two while I am still young enough to enjoy travel. It won't be first class, and if worst comes to worst I can always go back to selling.
>
> I am working on my memoirs at night and hope to finish it before I retire. People always have more respect for the man with a job.

Let us imagine an answer for the third writer, the self-made man.

> I am 65, retired from active service, but still serving on a number of boards. I think of these memoirs more as the story of building a successful business than as the story of my own life, although the two are much intertwined.
>
> Ten years ago I wouldn't dream of writing a book about myself, my business, or anything else, but now I realize that I have something to say, particularly to my children, and this is a very effective way of saying it.

The handicapped person might add,

> I find myself old at 44. Laughter is a rarity in my life. I look forward to visits to the doctor's office because it gives me a reason for getting up in the morning. I get an income from the money my parents left to care for me. It isn't much, but then I don't need much. I don't hate anyone, but at times I find myself bitter with God.

Now, let us get back to thinking about the outline. Having identified yourself and your motives for your reader, the next logical step is to tell him what you know about your ancestors. Remember they are also his.

Jot down the word "Ancestry." How far back can you trace your ancestry and the family name? When, why, and how did the family come to America? Do you have information on courtships and marriage of your parents? All this information and more should be in your notes.

Next you probably want to talk about your early memories, the houses you lived in, the neighbors. Did your adventures as a youngster shape any ideas for raising your own children later? How did you react to the other children in the family?

Does it seem logical to go to the grade school years next? It's up to you. It's your pile of notes and it's your life.

Just keep working away until each pile of notes has found a place in your outline, and your outline follows roughly your chronological life.

Be comforted with the thought that by the time you reach this stage you will know this book of yours like a book.

The following is a sample of an outline which is adequate to serve as a guide for organizing the final draft of one's memoirs. It is set up more or less chronographically, but has changed from dates to notes.

Date and *Who am I?*
Why am I writing this?
What is my situation at this time?
Ancestry
        Dad's memories leaving home for America
        Mom's memories leaving home for America
        Parents' courtship and marriage
        Move to Toledo
Memories of Linwood Avenue
        Elaborate on harmful effect of guilt feelings
Memories of Kent Street
        First experience with death
        Elaborate on changes in attitude toward death
The grade school years
        Elaborate on eyeglasses in the second grade
        Strong sense of justice in young people
        Living in shadow of sister
        Discovering downtown Toledo and freedom
        Influence of Newsboys Club and Boy Scouts

Commentary on how one's peers influence standards of behavior

The dry goods store

Observation that youngsters must not be expected to appreciate hard work of parents. Youngsters may feel that people who work hard want to work hard. Besides, for parents, hard work is the natural state.

How parents combatted the Great Depression

The high school years

Playmates vs. permanent friends

Introduction to the power of the press pass

Problems of the man-boy

The automobile

The university years

Love affair with the *Toledo Times*

Influence of certain professors

Early newspaper days

The work ethic

Love and marriage

Background on the wife and her family

The first meeting

The lapse

The courtship

The Cuban trip

The marriage

The fun and games days

Wild parties and thoughtlessness

The early World War II years

Military service

The training camps

Foreign Service

North Africa

Italy

Return to civilian life

The apprehension

Life at Twelfth and Jackson

Robert is born Jan. 30, 1947

Move to Lagrange Street

Raising the family
>   Betty is born August 12, 1950
>   The move to Cheltenham Road
>   The Ohio Cold Type Co.
> >   The struggle
> >   The survival
> >   The nice feeling of money
> >   Advantages and disadvantages of business for one's self
>   Educating the children
>   Robert and the Chinese
>   The romance and marriage of Bob and Ning
>   Betty and Larry married, Feb. 9, 1974
>   Betty and Larry divorced, 1979
>   Kevin, first grandchild born to Bob and Ning Aug. 10, 1975
>   Kori, second grandchild born May 19, 1981
>   Comment on life as grandparents

Meanwhile back to the newspaper
>   Covering sports
>   Feature writing and columning
>   Growing old in the job

Taking care of the parents
>   The nursing home years

Thoughts in closing
>   Religion
>   Issues of our times
> >   Prohibition
> >   Drugs
> >   Abortion
> >   Changes in mores
> >   Investing your money
>   Do what you can, ignore what you can't

The comfort of being old
>   Conclusion

Now let us examine the easier route to take. In this case you write or type your memoirs at random and put them in pages in what would be a rough chronological order.

It is important that you start out with the opening statements as described in the autobiographical method, explaining who you are, what your situation is, and why you are collecting your memoirs.

Insert your memoirs in a rough chronological order, and conclude with a message to the reader.

Review. In organizing your final manuscript you may go one or two routes: carefully assemble it in chronological order so that it will be more like an autobiography, or just insert isolated events as if in a photo album, in a roughly chronological order. The latter is far simpler.

In either case open with a statement of who you are, why you are leaving your memoirs, and what your situation is at the time you are writing them. The last item in the album should be sort of a farewell address to the reader.

XIII. Putting One Word After Another

*It's writing time, and with
the advice and encouragement
of this chapter, you should
find it a joy. If you think
that writing is difficult,
the chief task of this chapter
will be to convince you
you are wrong.*

The principal purpose of this chapter is to convince those who need such encouragement that it is not difficult to write well. It may turn out to be more of a pep talk than an instruction.

Think of your memoirs as a series of notes and letters to the reader you imagined in the previous chapter. The truth of the matter is that memoir writing is the easiest writing there is.

First, you are writing in the first person. *I* did this, and *I* thought this, and *I* saw this.

Second, you are the world's foremost expert on the subject— yourself.

Third, you have no editor, no publisher, no bookseller to please, and fourth, your readers are going to be so pleased with the idea of having a historic document near and dear to their hearts that they will appreciate it even though you write it upside down and backwards.

There is one more reason why writing is no problem in your memoirs. You have something to say. All this collecting of notes and ideas, all this talking with people, all this thinking you've done about your life story has given you plenty of substance, and you've got it all in your notes.

If a professional writer has something to say he says it. If he has nothing to say he tries to dazzle the readers with words. You needn't worry about this. You have something to say.

It may help if as you start to make each new segment you think to yourself, "Dear Jenny: Did I have a problem in 1968!!" Then, on paper you pick it up from there and start telling Jenny about the problem. Keep it simple. Keep it short. Write from the heart. Don't look up a single word in the dictionary. If the word isn't in your normal vocabulary, don't use it.

Now let us go on with this letter to "Jenny."

The most miserable period of my entire life came in the summer of 1968. Billy, just 3, came down with a very high fever and went into a coma. No one could seem to put a name to his problem, and all we could do was sit and look at his quiet little face and his still little arms, and pray.

Even in prayer there was no comfort. We lived only for test results. For awhile, as each test showed no problem in that area we were relieved, but after awhile I found myself becoming unreasonably angry with the tests. If there is nothing wrong why is he just lying there!

My poor husband not only had his sick little boy ever on his mind, but he also had to worry about a hysterical wife who was helping the situation not at all. I'd refused to take any medication the doctor offered for calming me down. "Will it cure Billy if I take it?" I would scream.

About the fourth day a nurse came up to me as I sat head down in a chair, pushed me roughly on the shoulder, and snarled, "Who are you feeling sorry for — yourself or your little boy?" I never heard of such a thing.

"Everybody who walks into this room cares more about that poor little boy than you do. They come in to help. Why are *you* here?"

Suddenly I didn't want to scratch her eyes out. What *had* I been doing?? "What *can* I do?" I asked her.

"I don't know," she said. "I'm not married anymore, but if I were I'd go home and have a hot plate of soup waiting for my husband when he came in."

My God, she was right. For the first time in days I didn't seem to mind walking into the house. I took some soup from the freezer and put it up to heat. I straightened things up. I looked in the cupboards to see what I needed.

That evening we talked for the first time about what we would do if Billy died. Life would go on, and it would drag us with it.

As it turned out they started seeing improvements in Billy's vital signs the next day, and in less than a month he was back to normal.

After that awful period any time I found myself facing some kind of a crisis I'd ask myself, "What are *you* doing here?" Then I'd look around for something useful to do.

There are a few writer's tricks in the above sample, but none that you cannot use yourself once they are called to your attention.

First there is the use of direct quotes. It breaks up the typography for one thing, and it can be used to emphasize a point for another.

Having the nurse say, "Who are you feeling sorry for — yourself or your little boy?" and having it set out in quotes is much more powerful that writing something like " — and then the nurse asked me who I was feeling sorry for, myself or my little boy."

Then you may notice the use of the phrase, "My God," in the sentence, "My God, she was right." It isn't necessary, but it gives the writing a conversational tone which is something good to achieve in an autobiography like this.

The best thing about the segment, and possibly the factor that most justifies including it in the biography is the fact that it ends up in a lesson which also serves as advice for the reader. It says, "Don't sit around and feel sorry for yourself if you can find something better to do."

There may be times when the language absolutely refuses to flow. Try writing in short sentences. It can be beautiful. Follow this commentary.

Age has its rewards. I was never comfortable with women. I didn't have the looks. I didn't have the muscle. I didn't have the nerve. I could teach violets how to be shy. I never kidded waitresses. I never told dirty jokes to barmaids. I was always polite. I cannot honestly say this is good. I was neglected a lot while better looking and more daring men were getting attention when they should have been getting slapped.

Now I dare to be charming. No longer do I have to be big and handsome. Just having my own hair is macho enough. Having my own teeth is a plus.

Another factor in writing which may tend to discourage some people is those two perils, spelling and grammar.

First let us take up the matter of spelling. Was it Mark Twain who said, "If Urop doesn't spell Europe what does it spell?" Well, no matter. The thought is a comforting one.

If you have had reasonable opportunity to have the spelling checked in your memoirs then it probably is wise to do so. The hyphenating guides are faster and easier to use than dictionaries in checking spelling.

If, however, your education necessarily was neglected for reasons of survival or some other good cause you may be able to give your descendant a more accurate picture of yourself by spelling in your own catch-as-catch-can style.

The problem of poor grammar is a bit harder to handle than poor spelling. If used it will reflect a bit of your true self to the reader. Whether that is good or bad depends upon whether you can justify this particular lack of knowledge. It might be well to have someone check your grammar out for you and make corrections as necessary.

Of course, if the character you've chosen for yourself is by nature careless and uneducated, it may be best to write in the language he would be likely to know best.

Punctuation, you will be happy to learn, is no exact science. Newspaper style books, for example, vary in their demands on uses of commas, colons, and semicolons. You may find the dash a useful device in punctuation. Let your instinct be your guide. When in doubt — dash.

There is now nothing between you and the end of your autobiography but the writing.

At this point it may be an idea to take a closer look at the album you acquired to bind your work for posterity. It is particularly versatile because while it will hold your written or typed pages, clippings, and photographs firmly, it also will permit you to rearrange your work easily. Simply lift the plastic cover, move the work around as you desire, and drop the cover again.

There is one more very useful thing you can do. If you wish to rewrite a paragraph or rearrange paragraphs, it is very simple. Merely cut the offending paragraph out with a scissors and insert the new paragraph. The adhesive back and the plastic cover will hold all pieces of paper firmly in place.

Follow your outline and your instincts, and you can't go wrong.

If you don't type, and feel uncomfortable with the readability of your handwriting, you have the alternative, of course, of having it typed. While public stenographers may be expensive, you might call the local university for typists who are likely to be more reasonable in cost. Students use such typing service for term papers.

XIV. Words to Remember By

This is a simple device for stimulating the mind and prodding the memory. Think of it as a challenge if you are alone and as a game if you are using it in groups.

Below is a list of more than 400 words selected to stimulate your thinking. Here's how to use them.

1. Select a word at random. The word suggests an area in our lives in which we have had to deal, in most cases indirectly.
2. Do you have an opinion relative to that area? Is it worth passing on to your future generations? Will it help their understanding of you and your times?
3. Was this opinion generated by something that happened in your life? Would you like to tell your readers about it?

The strategy of the exercise, of course, is to make you concentrate on the area suggested by the word until, hopefully, you find you do have an opinion and a reason for the opinion that may provide substance for your memoirs.

You may do this alone or with others. Nothing creates conversation like a firm opinion crisply voiced.

In actual practice any conversations inspired by one of these words quickly spread into other areas. Talk begets talk, memories beget memories. Don't worry about staying with the subject, just concentrate on keeping the talking, the opinionating, and the remembering going.

As a sample of inspiration, take the word, "Love."

Love was the greatest motivating force in my life. It was much greater than money. I know because when I had a choice of working overtime or going out with my wife-to-be, I always passed up the money, but it was the only time I gave up a chance for overtime pay.

I was told it wasn't wise from the legal point of view to have everything in both my wife's name and my own. My desire to share with her overshadowed my lawyer's common sense.

Once I told him, "If I keep everything in my name, I just know I'll give it all to her out of sheer love. By sharing it I get to keep at least half."

That's when he gave up on trying to advise me.

It now strikes me that I might point out that I come from a long line of successful marriages. Maybe if we'd paid more attention to money than love we'd have fewer successful marriages, but more successful businesses.

It's strange where dwelling on a word can take the mind.

abortion	atomic bomb	aging
religion	charity	patriotism
begging	marriage	crime and
avarice	divorce	punishment
pre-marital sex	travel	cheerfulness
living with illness	children	doctors
cash and credit	aliens	cheating
racial differences	strong drink	keeping busy
narcotics	coexistence	conceit
conflict	converts	congeniality
crusaders	curiosity	cynicism
damnation	debility	debts
danger	deceit	decadence
decency	self-delusion	democracy
discretion	dignity	discouragement

discipline	discussion	dogma
dreams	economy	education
ego	elections	endurance
envy	epitaphs	equality
exercise	extremism	failure
faith	fakery	family ties
fantasy	fascism	fellowship
fear	food	finances
fame	flirting	forgetfulness
freedom	fright	forgiveness
fortune-telling	free thinking	frigidity
funerals	gaiety	gambling
gaudiness	gentility	gladness
glamour	goodbyes	grandchildren
gloom	government	graybeards
graft	graves	grouches
greed	guns	guilt feelings
heaven	hair styles	hallucinations
hatred	happiness	headlines
headaches	overweight	underweight
heirs	helpfulness	heredity
heresy	The hereafter	hermits
history	hoarding	homeliness
honesty	homesickness	humaneness
humanity	hope	horses
homicide	homemaking	humor
honors	household pets	hunger
hunting	husbands	hypnosis
hysteria	hypochondria	idleness
ill-tempered	illogical	illness
imagination	immorality	impatience
importance	madness	magnetism
mail	male sex	malcontent
malignancy	manipulator	marijuana
malingerer	marriage	martyrdom
masculinity	mastermind	maturity
meddler	medication	melancholia
monogamy	monopoly	moodiness

morale	morbidity	mortality
motherhood	medicare	mediocrity
melodrama	melody	memorials
memory	menus	mentality
mercy	merchandising	merriment
The Messiah	middle age	middle class
modesty	militarism	millionaires
minorities	metric system	modernization
money	molestation	might
mercenaries	motivation	mudslinging
music	mutiny	mysticism
nagging	names	Narcissism
naivete	nationalism	neatness
narrow-mindedness	negativism	news
nostalgia	nudism	objectivity
objectors	obsessions	obstacles
occultism	offensiveness	obstructionist
orderliness	opinions	opportunism
omens	overawe	pacemakers
parenthood	panic	pain
parsimony	partnership	partisanship
patronizing	peace	pedigree
penitence	peers	pennywise
perfection	persecution	personality
peril	perversion	persistence
pessimism	pettiness	plainness
physique	pity	plausibility
pleasantries	poetry	politics
popularity	pornography	posivitism
potentiality	prayer	predictability
poverty	pretending	privilege
productivity	profanity	promiscuity
promotion	prosperity	prostitution
psychiatry	punishment	quackery
quaintness	qualms	rashness
reactionary	readability	rebellion
reasonableness	radio	rape
rationalizing	realism	remembering

reliability
repression
restraint
risk-taking
romance
rumors
sacrifice
safety
sarcasm
scheming
seashore
second-hand
self-defense
senselessness
serenity
servants
sharing
short tempers
shyness
sisterhood
slander
solicitousness
soreheads
soul
starvation
stealth
stinginess
strikes
suavity
suicide
superficiality
superstitions
sweatshops
sympathy
tardiness
taxes
teases
telephones

rebirths
reprimand
retaliation
reverence
robots
runaways
sadness
sales
scandal
schools
seduction
self-pity
self-control
sensitivity
sensuality
sewing
shopping
showiness
sight
sin
slavery
solitaire
sororities
space age
statesmen
stepchildren
stock market
straightforward
style
sunshine
supermarkets
surgery
sweets
talebearer
taste
taxis
teenagers
tension

remorse
rent
retribution
reunions
royalty
sabbath
sadism
sameness
scapegoat
scriptures
security
self-education
senility
sentimentality
servitude
shame
shortages
sickliness
silence
skepticism
sleep
sophism
sorrow
spendthrifts
statistics
sterility
straight-faced
stupidity
suffering
Sundays
supernatural
survival
swindles
temper
tattling
tears
television
terror

thanksgiving
therapy
tiredness
tolerance
tranquility
trivia
truth
usefulness
vegetating
vice
visitors
wealth
windfalls
wordiness

theater
thievery
tobacco
tomorrow
treachery
trouble
trustworthiness
Utopia
ventilation
villainy
vulgarity
weather
window-shopping
youth

theology
timidity
togetherness
tranquilizers
treason
troublemakers
union
vanity
victory
vindication
wakefulness
wives
writing

XV. Wrapping It Up
and Putting It Away

*Your manuscript is finished
and you now must prepare it
for posterity. This chapter has
some ideas on the subject.*

You have now committed your memoirs to paper. You've told all you plan to tell, and you are ready to assemble the whole thing in its final resting place in the self-adhesive photo album.

The thoughts start pouring in. Will one copy of your autobiography be enough? To whom will you give it? How can you ascertain that it will be passed on to future generations?

Maybe you don't want to wait until you are dead before it is read? It might be fun being around while it is made public.

Needless to say, there are several answers to each of these questions. Let us consider some of them.

The simplest answer to the first four questions is where there is a will, there is a way. You put all your requirements in your will. The executor will be in charge of seeing that the manuscript goes to the person you designate. You may designate a date before which you do not wish it to be opened and read. You may designate that it will be passed on through the eldest child of each generation. Of course your wishes may not be carried out, but you can be certain of two things. First, you'll never know, and second, after the first generation your memoirs will be a valuable curio and a treasure.

If you feel the need for more than one copy and you are disinclined to pay the costs, you may request that the executor see to it that additional copies be made and distributed. The cost, of course, would have to come from your estate.

Actually, you are not talking about a great deal of money. Copies may be made on copy machines for as little as 5 cents per page or $5 for the 100 pages. Then there is the matter of buying additional photo albums and inserting the pages. Total cost may be as little as $15 per book. Each book distributed enhances your chances of making it big in posterity. You know, they may make great Christmas gifts.

You may make up several copies to be distributed to your heirs at the time of your death, and expressing the wish in your will that each passes the copy on to the heir of his choice with a similar wish for perpetuating its existence.

Granting the above options exist, let's take a good practical look at the situation. You don't really have to make it part of a will. Give it to someone you love and trust, and tell him what you have in mind. Then hope for the best. There's a very good chance that if you should return to earth 100 years from now, your book will be here to greet you. The idea of passing family heirlooms down, and that's what your book will be, is pretty well established in our society — and this heirloom you don't have to worry about someone pawning.

A rather prominent man once let word get out that he was killed abroad in an automobile accident. He returned home shortly afterward, and admitted that the whole thing was a hoax. He hadn't even been abroad. He did it to find out how his death would be accepted. He couldn't stand not knowing.

What does that have to do with us?

Is it possible that you can't stand not knowing how your autobiography will be received? Do you want to have some more fun with it?

Even assuming you've written it with the idea that it would not be read in your lifetime, it may be worth the little risk involved for the attention it would gain for you. Can you imagine the tidbits of conversation?

"Mother! How could you write such a thing about me????"
"Shut up, darling, or I'll make it even worse."

"Myrtle, that isn't at all true about me!" "Oh, I just put it in to shake you up. I'm going to take it out." "But what if you were killed in an auto accident before you got around to it?" "You'll drive carefully taking me home tonight."

Those situations are exaggerated, of course, assuming you were reasonable, honest and accurate and charitable in your writing, but there is little question that you'd be getting more attention than you've had in a long time. You might even be asked to help others with their memoirs.

There is one more thing you may care to do with your work. You may offer a copy to the local history organization in your community, generally associated with the public library. In such case it may be wise to stipulate a length of time before it becomes public.

Finally, you are completely finished. You've written your whole life story, and you've still got some life left over. What to do? What to do?

No problem. Write a sequel. Some authors have made careers out of writing sequels to first great books.

XVI. Excerpts from One Man's Memoirs

*This chapter will give
you some idea of what
your finished product
may look like, and how
it may read.*

*(This is the opening statement, and it covers the time, place, and
mental and physical state of the writer, and hints of a bit of sensitivity in writing about himself.)*

My name is Robert Cornwood, and I am pleased that you are
interested enough in this document to peruse it. The year is 1987.
I live in Toledo, Ohio, U.S.A. I am 70, and still sensible enough
to feel a bit confused as to why I am writing my memoirs.

I assume this document will be read by my children and their
children. Yet, I am trying to write this for the generations of the
future that I will never know, and who will know me only by what
I have to say here. Being an introvert by nature, I am having some
difficulty handling it. I can only hope it becomes easier as I go
along.

The two words that best describe me at this time of life are *contented* and *grateful*. I live in a comfortable apartment, have few
responsibilities, and seem to have adapted well to being old. The
truth of the matter is I don't feel at all old. Sometimes I use my
advanced years as an excuse for not doing things, but I never really
feel that I can't do them.

A strange thing is that I feel better off than any of my aging friends. I suspect that this comes with age. They probably feel better off than I am. What probably is really happening is that all of us feel lucky to find that 70 isn't really so old after all.

At this point in my life, money is no problem. Health is no problem. Only fear of the future is a problem, and I solve that one by not thinking about it.

To give you an idea of my world, we are just getting into the computer age. My memoirs are being written on a PC, a personal computer. It has replaced the typewriter for most of us who do any great amount of writing. The military is doing a great deal with computers to make weapons more powerful and accurate.

Travel is largely by jet planes which fly considerably over 500 miles per hour. We do have a passenger plane that will break the sound barrier, but passage is very expensive so it is not used much.

The use of the satellite to beam radio signals around the world has become commonplace, and radio and television have replaced the newspapers as gatherers of spot news. Newspapers, however, remain important because they handle the news in greater depth.

The world's big problem seems to be small groups of terrorists who make token attacks in airports and urban areas leaving a lot of uninvolved people maimed or dead. A policy on how to deal with and thwart these people is forming, but it involves a lot of trial and error. Except that it makes unpleasant reading and does discourage travel in some parts of the world, particularly the Middle East.

Now it is time for me to forget about the world and to write about me, my experiences, and my thoughts.

Now starts the memoirs. The author elects to start with his earliest memories, and to weave family background into the memoirs as he goes along. The reason seems to be that he doesn't really have enough family background. Someone who can trace his family back some distance may prefer to tell where his family comes from.

My first memory of this life goes back, I believe, to when I was a three-year-old. My father had a small delivery truck used to deliver laundry. I think they called the process "wet-wash." The clothing would be delivered still damp and ready for pressing by the housewife. I seem to remember the fresh smell of clean laundry.

As I remember it, the truck had no doors. It was designed so that driver and helper could leap in and out easily. I very definitely remember my mother clutching me to her breast as we'd ride in it. I never worried about falling out. It may have been the trust and security the very young seem to have for their parents.

The one very distinct memory I have of this period is my father helping my mother canning something in glass jars and a jar breaking in his hand and cutting it badly. My Dad cried out in pain and I was rushed from the room.

Eventually, I returned, but I didn't want to look at my father or to talk to him. I have yet to figure that one out. I like to think it was because he had hurt someone I loved, but I suspect the real reason was an aversion to blood.

A throwaway thought.

These days I often find myself wondering if I was as good a father as my father was. I know that he had to face a lot more adversity than I did, so he may have been a better man, but was he a better father? My honest answer is, I have no idea.

There is a lesson in this memoir. In a subtle way Mr. Cornwood is advising his readers to get to know their parents better even if it means getting a little bit intimate with them.

As I write my memoirs I can't get over how little I actually know about my parents. The image they left with me was that they were both very good people.

Obviously they slept together. They did have two children, but I can't remember ever seeing them being even a little bit, shall we say, over-familiar.

On rare occasions Dad would use a swear word, usually in Hungarian, but I don't recall his ever making an off-color remark or telling an off-color story—and I was 65 when he died.

Now, my common sense tells me that this was not his natural state. He worked in the factories and in the garment centers where vulgarisms were as much a part of the business as buttonholes. All I can think is that our relationship never reached the point where he felt he could treat me like an adult.

Come to think of it, I never told an off-color story in his presence either. It's too bad we didn't get to know each other better.

The statement below deals with an attitude toward school and authority. As you will see, the statement is based on actual past incidents which form a lesson provided by experience.

From kindergarten to my final year at the university, I attended school with the same discipline that I later attended work. The idea of not going to school, or even playing hookey, never occurred to me. I can't say if it was the serious attitude my parents took toward education or if it was my fear of being punished.

It well could have been the latter. I may have inherited it from my Dad, who very definitely showed signs of fear of authority. In this case I can understand it.

Dad was raised in Hungary where, for a Jew, anyone in uniform including a mailman was an object to be feared. He told me that once when he was a boy, soldiers came through his town, broke into homes, and took whatever food and most livestock they could find.

When the people marched to the mayor's house to complain, the mayor said he'd lodged a very strong protest with the officer in charge.

The reply was, "Who told them to let the soldiers take the stuff?!"

As a young adult I was in a position to fix an occasional traffic ticket. On the rare occasion that my father would get a ticket, he would refuse to let me take care of it. He insisted on paying it. With money as scarce as it was in those days, I'm sure this came more from a fear of complications with the authorities that it did from good citizenship.

Possibly to break up the page Mr. Cornwood occasionally inserted short thoughts between his longer passages.

As a university student I once challenged a professor with the question "How do you grade me, by what I know or by how much I have learned?"

"I grade you according to what will be most helpful to you. If you are a lazy student, I give you a low grade to make you work harder. If you are dedicated to your studies I give you a high grade to encourage you. I don't give grades to reward you. If I thought good grades were a reward I'd give you lollipops instead."

Below is a memoir dealing with prejudices. It contains a rather valuable lesson in understanding people.

There were just two children in the family. I had a sister, Alma, who was four years older. As I think back I can see that we were rivals in the family, but outside we were very supportive of each other.

In later years I saw this recur at many levels in life. I could say what was wrong with my school, but let an outsider say something nasty about it and he had an argument on his hands. I could criticize my boss, but let an outsider be critical and I went to the boss's support.

I finally figured out that this is the way people think. The right to criticize a group is recognized only by the people within the group. In later life, unless I was deliberately trying to provoke an argument, I never attacked the medical profession while talking to a doctor, or the legal profession while talking to a lawyer.

I once was talking with an elderly woman who had accomplished a great deal in elevating the status of blacks long before civil rights were even considered an issue. I admired her greatly, and was expressing some displeasure at the attitude of whites when she stopped me.

"It isn't that they are white," she corrected, "it is that we are strangers. I was raised in West Virginia among whites. My playmates were white. I didn't know what prejudice was until I left home to go to the university. I think the human animal finds it very difficult to hate someone he knows without a very definite reason. When blacks hate whites and whites hate blacks, they are hating the ones they don't know."

The following is an example of an idea about life brought on by experience.

In my times cancer is the big health problem. Vast amounts of money are collected each year to finance research and treatment. I am perfectly in accord with this. Yet, it seems that they are finding more causes than cures.

Sometimes I find myself doubting the sincerity of the whole cause. The more people can be frightened the more they will contribute. It seems that of late we have been told that everything we say, do, eat or look at may cause cancer. A person could die of a heart attack worrying about what might be causing cancer.

Some day I'm going to issue a bumper sticker that says, "Giving to cancer drives may cause cancer," but I doubt if I'll have the nerve to put one on my car. It may cause violence.

The disease I fear the most these days is Alzheimer's disease. It attacks the brain in the aged, and seems to cause a return to infancy and worse. Some of my older friends have been victims, and I can't believe the results. If anyone ever starts a fund for Alzheimer's, they won't have to worry about me issuing bumper stickers.

The following statement can be justified because it tells about the times as well as the writer. Who will believe there was a time we didn't have television?

Some years ago a student in one of my writing classes wrote, "Gadget Lovers of America: I married your king." I gave her a good grade, but she was wrong. My wife married their king.

Gadgets are my weakness. I was among the first reporters to have a police radio in my car back in 1936. The police had a one-way system at the time, and the one radio got all the emergency calls. I was courting my wife at the time, and she finally got so she wouldn't get into the car unless I turned it off. She was tired of going to fires.

I mean, considering that I never owned a first-class tennis racquet, a good set of golf woods, a bowling ball drilled to fit, a pool cue or a new baseball glove because I couldn't justify the cost, it seems I could have resisted the temptation for getting these even more expensive gadgets, but I could not. I still can't.

I was among the first in my set to have a crystal radio, a portable radio, an automatic transmission in my car, a television set, a portable tape recorder, a citizen's band receiver, a portable electric organ, a wireless telephone, a police scanner, a personal portable computer and a videorecorder. At the moment I am trying to get up nerve to buy a camcorder.

That first portable tape recorder was about as portable as your average anvil. It was built like a large suitcase, and weighed at least 25 pounds. It needed all the electricity one could find to run it, and could not be used with batteries.

One time I used it to interview the president of Western Reserve University in Cleveland. It turned out that he had a similar one that he used in arbitrations, so we had immediate rapport.

"I wouldn't go to an arbitration without one," he confided. "I put it in the middle of the table so everyone knows it's there. Suddenly everyone becomes much more careful of what they say and how they say it and we get the thing over much faster. I really use it more to keep the peace than to keep a record."

Through the years I found this to be true of the smaller portables I used in interviews later. While the subject seems to forget the tape recorder is there after I show him how it works and invite him to turn it off anytime he likes, no one with whom I've recorded an interview ever denied that he said what I quoted him saying.

Religion has been with us for a long time, and it seems it is here to stay in one form or another. All memoirs should have some comment on that subject.

I wonder what religion will be like in your time. In my time I saw it move from a vital part of my life to a relatively unimportant something that I accept more for tradition's sake than as a necessity.

I have a feeling that I never was truly religious. As a youngster I practiced religion because of my parents. As a father I participated in it even more fully because of the children. Now that I am old I remain attached to it, I believe, so that I can be buried with my own people.

The crazy thing here is that I see no advantage to being buried with friends—but I hate the thought of being buried among strangers.

I must admit that for all the evils committed in the name of religion, it has been very important in civilizing the human race. Originally it wisely used superstition and fear of a god or gods to make us accept some sort of law. Then, as mass ignorance disappeared, it started appealing to the better nature of the human animal.

Actually it has been more successful than we tend to admit. We walk through life today among men much more physical than we are, yet we assume, correctly in most cases, that they will make no effort to take our possessions from us.

Here's a throwaway thought to break up the type.

During my time in military service I noticed that in time of stress many men sought to express their feelings in writing, frequently in poetry. The classic was when we were on a troopship during a storm in the Atlantic and thought we were being followed by German submarines, one of the men passed around two lines he'd written,

Get me off this boat, my frien',
And I will never float again.

It broke the tension, got a lot of us talking and laughing, and as far as I'm concerned it's the greatest two lines of poetry I've ever known.

Here Mr. Cornwood tries to wrap up all his memoirs with a philosophy of life and a message to his readers.

There's an old nightclub line that comes to mind at this time—*If I had it to do all over again, I'd do it all over you.* Obviously it is an inane and maybe even sickening line, yet it describes my attitude toward self-criticism at my time in life completely.

If I had it to do all over again, what would I do differently? I honestly don't know. I've made some mistakes but some of the most enjoyable times in my life came while I was making mistakes. For example, it may have been a mistake to go out with a girl five years younger than me, but I wound up marrying her, raising a family with her, and getting old with her. I wouldn't trade that mistake for all the right things to do described in the Bible.

I may have made a mistake staying in one city all my life. I might have done better in New York, but how much better do I need? If a man is contented, should he be concerned that with a little more effort he might have been joyous?

I'm certain that being satisfied with my lot cut into my ambition, but I loved my lot, and to me that's all that is necessary. I have won life's struggle, do I want to try for double or nothing. It's good to want to achieve more and better, but if you can achieve it without wanting to achieve it it's even better. The pain of wanting frequently is not worth the satisfaction of achieving.

Personally, I consider my life a success. I was never wealthy so I always had the chase for the dollar to keep me from being bored. I was never particularly strong, so there was no great demand for the use of my back or muscle. I was never ambitious, so that spared me a lot of jealousy.

Let me close with what I consider the most important attribute in my life—the ability to forget. I had the ability to control my mind so that I could dismiss from it whatever I liked. I did not stew over past mistakes. I did not worry about things over which I had no control. I could concentrate on a problem at hand, or I could dismiss it from my mind until a more opportune time to take it up.

Now comes the time we have all been waiting for, the time to conclude one's memoirs. Oddly enough, you needn't wait until you are through writing your memoirs to write this. Write as soon as you know what you want to say. That way there's no danger of leaving this earth before you have the opportunity to say it.

I think I know how George Washington felt when he bade farewell to his troops. This is a farewell message to a world I'll never know. I wonder if people feel this way when they write suicide notes?

Of course, I know as I write this that there are still some good years left. I like to think that they'll be the best years. I even know that if I care to add anything to my memoirs even after this is written, there is nothing or no one to stop me. Yet, I must assume that this will be the last thing you will read of my memoirs, therefore it must have a satisfactory closing.

I have high hopes that as a result of my writing you now know me better than even most of my friends did, and that you kind of like me. I'm really hoping you'll think that I was a pretty wise old bird who knew how to enjoy life—something like Benjamin Franklin, maybe—and was lucky enough to be given every opportunity to take advantage of it. I also hope that the world in which you are living has learned to distribute its wealth of food and creature comforts, to get along without wars and terrorism, and to eliminate diseases and illness.

I also hope that there remain enough problems to be solved and goals to be reached to keep life from becoming boring.

Having spent a great deal of pleasant time and effort in producing this document, I find myself wondering if anyone will ever read it. One thought encourages me. If my great-grandfather had written his memoirs, I'd certainly read them.

Index

19.45